THE COOK'S ENCYCLOPEDIA OF

BARBECUES, GRILLS & OUTDOOR EATING

THE COOK'S ENCYCLOPEDIA OF

BARBECUES, GRILLS & OUTDOOR EATING

CONTRIBUTING EDITOR: CHRISTINE FRANCE

LORENZ BOOKS

This edition published in 2001 by Lorenz Books
27 West 20th Street, New York, NY 10011

LORENZ BOOKS are available for bulk purchase for sales promotion
and for premium use. For details, write or call the sales director,
Lorenz Books, 27 West 20th Street, New York, NY 10011

www.lorenzbooks.com

Publisher: Joanna Lorenz
Project Editor: Sarah Ainley
Copy Editor: Beverley Jollands
Designer: Nigel Partridge
Illustrations: Madeleine David and Lucinda Ganderton
Photographers: Karl Adamson, William Adams-Lingwood, Edward Allwright,
Steve Baxter, James Duncan, John Freeman, Michelle Garrett, Amanda Heywood,
Don Last, Michael Michaels, Patrick McLeavey, Debbie Patterson and Juliet Piddington
Recipes: Carla Capalbo, Jacqueline Clark, Carole Clements, Roz Denny, Nicola Diggins, Tessa
Evelegh, Joanna Farrow, Christine France, Silvana Franco, Soheila Kimberley,
Ruby Le Bois, Sue Maggs, Katherine Richmond, Steven Wheeler and Elizabeth Wolf-Cohen

Previously published as *The Ultimate Barbecue Cookbook*

Printed and bound in China

3 5 7 9 10 8 6 4 2

CONTENTS

• • •

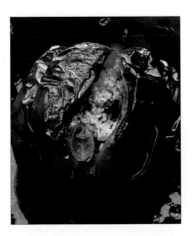

INTRODUCTION

———⊷◆⊶———

However simple, there's something about the charbroiled flavor of barbecued food that makes it taste extra special. Maybe it owes part of its appeal to the fresh air that sharpens the appetite and makes that tantalizing aroma so totally irresistible.

There's nothing new about cooking over charcoal; in fact, it's a method of cooking that has been used in most civilizations throughout history. The basic method has changed little over the centuries, but many modern grills are very sophisticated, making the job easier, cleaner and more controllable. Whether you're cooking over a simple pile of sticks or on a state-of-the art gas grill, outdoor cooking is fun, easy and inexpensive.

There are disputes over the origin of the word "barbecue," but one explanation is that it comes from *barbacoa*, a Spanish-American word used by the Arawak tribe of the Caribbean as the name for the wooden frame that held their food over an open fire as it cooked. The Arawaks were cannibals, so the food we cook today is rather different from their offerings!

Whatever your tastes, this collection of recipes offers new, unusual ideas for your barbecue as well as some traditional favorites. There's something for every occasion, from family meals to entertaining: spicy, fruity and exotic grills using fish, meat and poultry; easy sauces and marinades to turn basic ingredients into something new and special; and luscious, indulgent desserts. For vegetarians, there's a whole chapter of innovative ideas that everyone will enjoy.

Best of all, not only does a barbecue set the cook free from the kitchen but, for once, everyone else will actually want to help with the cooking.

CHOOSING A GRILL

. . .

There is a huge choice of ready-made grills on the market, and it's important to choose one that suits your particular needs. First decide how many people you want to cook for and where you are likely to use the grill. For instance, do you usually have barbecues just for the family, or are you likely to have barbecue parties for lots of friends? Once you've decided on your basic requirements, you will be able to choose between the different types more easily.

ABOVE: *Hibachis*

Hibachis

These small cast-iron grills originated in Japan—the word *hibachi* translates literally as "firebox." They are inexpensive, easy to use and easily transportable. Lightweight versions are now made in steel or aluminum.

Disposable Grills

These will last for about an hour and are a convenient idea for picnic-style barbecues or for cooking just a few small pieces of food.

Portable Grills

These are usually quite light and fold away to fit into a car trunk so you can take them on picnics. Some are even small enough to fit into a backpack.

Brazier Grills

These open grills are suitable for use on a patio or in the garden. Most have legs or wheels, and it's a good idea to check that the height suits you. The grill

LEFT: Brazier grill
BELOW: Disposable grill
RIGHT: Portable grill

area of a brazier varies in size, and the brazier may be round or rectangular. It's useful to choose one that has a shelf attached to the side. Other extras may include an electric, battery-powered or clockwork spit: Choose one on which you can adjust the height of the spit. Many brazier grills have a hood, which is useful as a windbreak and gives a place to mount the spit.

ordinary house bricks, but it's best to line the inside with firebricks, which will withstand the heat better. Use a metal shelf for the fuel and a grid at whatever height you choose. Kits are available containing all you need to build a grill.

ABOVE: Improvised grill

Improvised Grills

Barbecue cooking adds to the fun of eating outdoors on picnics and camping, trips but transporting the grill for the rest of the day can make the idea more of a chore than a treat. Basic grills can be built at almost no cost and can be dismantled after use as quickly as they were put together. A pile of stones topped with chicken wire and fueled with driftwood or kindling makes a very efficient grill. Or take a large cookie tin with you and punch a few holes in it; fill it with charcoal and place a grid on top. With just a little planning, you can turn your trip into a truly memorable event.

ABOVE: Gas grill

Kettle Grills

These have a large, hinged lid, which can be used as a windbreak; when closed, the lid allows you to use the grill rather like an oven. Even large cuts of meat or whole turkeys cook successfully, as the heat reflected within the dome helps to brown the meat evenly. The heat is easily controlled by the use of efficient air vents. This type of grill can also be used for home-smoking foods.

Gas Grills

The main advantage of these is their convenience—the heat is instant and easily controllable. The disadvantage is that they tend to be quite expensive.

Permanent Grills

These are a good idea if you often have barbecues at home. They can be built simply and cheaply. Choose a sheltered site that is a little way from the house, but with easy access to the kitchen. Permanent grills can be built with

ABOVE: Permanent grill

TYPES OF FUEL

· · ·

If you have a gas or electric grill, you will not need to buy extra fuel, but other grills require either charcoal or wood. Be sure to choose good-quality fuel and always remember to store it in a dry place.

Lump Charcoal
Lump charcoal is usually made from softwood, and comes in lumps of varying size. It is easier to ignite than briquettes, but tends to burn up faster.

Charcoal Briquettes
Briquettes are a cost-effective choice of fuel, as they burn for a long time with a minimum of smell and smoke. They can take a long time to ignite, however.

ABOVE: Charcoal briquettes

Self-Igniting Charcoal
This is simply lump charcoal or briquettes treated with a flammable substance that catches fire very easily. It's important to wait until the ignition agent has burned off before cooking food, or the smell may taint the food.

Coconut-Shell Charcoal
This makes a good fuel for small grills. It's best used on a fire grate with small holes, as the small pieces tend to fall through the gaps.

Wood
Hardwoods such as oak and olive are best for grilling, as they burn slowly, with a pleasant aroma. Softwoods tend to burn too fast and give off sparks and smoke, making them unsuitable for most grills. Wood fires need constant attention to achieve an even, steady heat.

CONTROLLING THE HEAT
There are three basic ways to control the heat of the grill during cooking.

1 Adjust the height of the grill rack. Raise it for slow cooking, or use the bottom level for searing foods. For medium heat, the rack should be about four inches from the fire.

2 Push the burning coals apart for lower heat; pile them closer together to increase the heat of the fire.

3 Most grills have air vents to allow air into the fire. Open them to make the fire hotter, or close them to lower the temperature.

Wood Chips and Herbs
These are designed to be added to the fire to impart a pleasant aroma to the food. They can be soaked to make them last longer. Scatter wood chips and herbs straight onto the coals during cooking, or place them on a metal tray under the grill rack. Packs of hickory or oak chips are easily available, or you can simply scatter twigs of juniper, rosemary, thyme, sage or fennel over the fire.

LIGHTING THE FIRE
Follow these basic instructions for lighting the fire unless you are using self-igniting charcoal, in which case you should follow the manufacturer's instructions.

1 Spread a layer of foil over the base of the grill, to reflect the heat and make cleaning easier.

2 Spread a layer of wood, charcoal or briquettes on the fire grate about two inches deep. Pile the fuel in a small pyramid in the center.

3 Push one or two lighters into the fuel or pour about three tablespoons of lighting fluid over it and let sit for 1 minute. Light with a long match or taper and allow to burn for 15 minutes. Spread the coals evenly and leave them to heat for 30–45 minutes, until they are covered with a film of gray ash, before cooking.

BELOW: Lump charcoal

BELOW: Coconut-shell charcoal

SAFETY TIPS

• • •

Barbecuing is a perfectly safe method of cooking if it's done sensibly—use these simple guidelines as a basic checklist to safeguard against accidents. If you have never organized a barbecue before, keep your first few attempts as simple as possible, with just one or two types of food. When you have mastered the technique of cooking on a grill you can start to become more ambitious. Soon you will progress from burgers for two to meals for large parties of family and friends.

☆ Make sure the grill is sited on a firm surface and is stable and level before lighting the fire. Once the grill is lit, do not move it.

☆ Keep the grill sheltered from the wind, and keep it well away from trees and shrubs.

☆ Always follow the manufacturer's instructions for your grill, as there are some grills that can use only one type of fuel.

☆ Don't try to speed up the fire—some fuels may take a long time to build up heat. Never pour flammable liquid onto the grill.

☆ Keep children and pets away from the fire and make sure the cooking is always supervised by adults.

☆ Keep perishable foods cold until you're ready to cook—especially in hot weather. If you take them outdoors, place them in a cool bag until needed.

☆ Make sure meats such as burgers, sausages and poultry are thoroughly cooked—there should be no trace of pink in the juices. Pierce a thick part of flesh as a test: the juices should run clear.

RIGHT: Poultry can be precooked in the oven or microwave before being finished off on the grill

ABOVE: Light the fire with a long match or taper, and leave it to burn for about 15 minutes

☆ Wash your hands after handling raw meat and before touching other foods. Don't use the same utensils for raw ingredients and cooked food.

☆ You may prefer to precook poultry in the microwave or oven and then transfer it to the grill to finish cooking and to attain the flavor of barbecued food. Don't allow meat to cool down before transferring it to the grill; poultry should never be reheated once it has already cooled.

☆ In case the fire should get out of control, have a bucket of sand and a water spray on hand to douse the flames.

☆ Keep a first-aid kit handy. If someone gets burnt, hold the burn under cold running water.

☆ Trim excess fat from meat and don't use too much oil in marinades. Fat can cause dangerous flare-ups if too much is allowed to drip onto the fuel.

☆ Use long-handled grilling tools, such as forks, tongs and brushes, for turning and basting food; keep some oven gloves nearby, preferably the extra-long type, to protect your hands.

☆ Always keep the raw foods to be cooked away from foods that are ready to eat, to prevent cross-contamination.

BASIC TIMING GUIDE

· · ·

It is almost impossible to give precise timing guides for barbecuing, as there are so many factors to consider. The heat will depend on the type and size of the grill, the type of fuel used, the height of the rack above the fire and, of course, the weather. Cooking times will also be affected by the thickness and type of food, the quality of the meat, and where on the grill it is placed.

Bearing this in mind, the chart below provides only a rough guide to timing. Food should always be tested to make sure it is thoroughly cooked. The times given here are total cooking times, allowing for the food to be turned. Most foods need turning only once, but smaller items, such as kebabs and sausages, need to be turned more frequently to ensure even cooking. Foods wrapped in foil cook more slowly and will need longer on the grill.

Type of Food	Weight/ Thickness	Heat	Total Cooking Time
Beef			
steaks	1 inch	hot	rare: 5 minutes
			medium: 8 minutes
			well done: 12 minutes
burgers	¾ inch	hot	6–8 minutes
kebabs	1 inch	hot	5–8 minutes
roasts	3½ pounds	spit	2–3 hours
Lamb			
leg steaks	¾ inch	medium	10–15 minutes
chops	1 inch	medium	10–15 minutes
kebabs	1 inch	medium	6–15 minutes
butterfly leg	3 inches	low	rare: 40–45 minutes
			well done: 1 hour
rolled shoulder	3½ pounds	spit	1¼–1½ hours
Pork			
chops	1 inch	medium	15–18 minutes
kebabs	1 inch	medium	12–15 minutes
spareribs		medium	30–40 minutes
sausages	thick	medium	8–10 minutes
roasts	3½ pounds	spit	2–3 hours

Type of Food	Weight/ Thickness	Heat	Total Cooking Time
Chicken			
whole	3½ pounds	spit	1–1¼ hours
quarters		medium	30–35 minutes
boneless breasts		medium	10–15 minutes
drumsticks		medium	25–30 minutes
kebabs		medium	6–10 minutes
poussin, whole	1 pound	spit	25–30 minutes
poussin, split	1 pound	medium	25–30 minutes
Duckling			
whole	5 pounds	spit	1–1½ hours
half		medium	35–45 minutes
breasts, boneless		medium	15–20 minutes
Fish			
large, whole	5–10 pounds	low/ medium	allow 10 minutes per 1 inch thickness
small, whole	1¼–2 pounds	hot/ medium	12–20 minutes
sardines		hot/ medium	4–6 minutes
steaks or fillets	1 inch	medium	6–10 minutes
kebabs	1 inch	medium	5–8 minutes
large shrimp in shell		medium	6–8 minutes
large shrimp, shelled		medium	4–6 minutes
scallops/mussels in shell		medium	until open
scallops/mussels, shelled, skewered		medium	5–8 minutes
half lobster		low/ medium	15–20 minutes

MARINATING

• • •

Marinades are used to add flavor and to moisten or tenderize foods, particularly meat. Marinades can be either savory or sweet and are as varied as you want to make them: spicy, fruity, fragrant or exotic. Certain classic combinations always work well with certain foods. Usually, it is best to choose oily marinades for dry foods, such as lean meat or white fish, and wine- or vinegar-based marinades for rich foods with a higher fat content. Most marinades don't contain salt, which can draw out the juices from meat. It's better to add salt just before, or after, cooking.

1 Place the food for marinating in a wide, nonmetallic dish or bowl, preferably a dish that is large enough to allow the food to lie in a single layer.

2 Mix together the ingredients for the marinade according to the recipe. The marinade can usually be prepared in advance and stored in a jar with a screw-top lid until needed.

Cook's Tip
The amount of marinade you will need depends on the amount of food. As a rough guide, about 2/3 cup is enough for about 1¼ pounds of food.

3 Pour the marinade over the food and turn the food to coat it evenly.

4 Cover the dish or bowl with plastic wrap and chill in the refrigerator for anywhere from 30 minutes up to several hours or overnight, depending on the recipe. Turn the food over occasionally, and spoon the marinade over it to make sure it is well coated.

5 Remove the food with a slotted spoon, or lift it out with tongs, and drain off and reserve the marinade. If necessary, allow the food to come to room temperature before cooking.

6 Use the marinade for basting or brushing the food during cooking.

BELOW: *Marinating foods before cooking adds to the flavor and ensures the food is kept tender and moist*

BASIC BARBECUE MARINADE
This can be used for meat or fish.

1 garlic clove, crushed
3 tablespoons sunflower or olive oil
3 tablespoons dry sherry
1 tablespoon Worcestershire sauce
1 tablespoon dark soy sauce
freshly ground black pepper

RED WINE MARINADE
This is good with red meats and game.

2/3 cup dry red wine
1 tablespoon olive oil
1 tablespoon red wine vinegar
2 garlic cloves, crushed
2 dried bay leaves, crumbled
freshly ground black pepper

APPETIZERS AND SNACKS

As everyone knows, there is nothing like the aroma of charbroiling food

to whet the appetite. To keep your guests happy while they are waiting

for the main event, begin your barbecue feast with exciting appetizers

that are quick to cook and fun to eat. Here is a collection of

flavorsome and colorful dishes that are guaranteed to disappear

from the grill rack as soon as they're cool enough to snatch away.

There are lots of creative recipes for finger foods to be nibbled with

drinks – from crisp potato skins to spicy spare ribs – with plenty of

interesting dips and sauces to dunk them in, as well as delicious

suggestions for elegant appetizers for more formal meals.

ROASTED GARLIC TOASTS

• • •

Roasting garlic in its skin on a grill produces a soft, aromatic purée with a sweet, nutty flavor.
Spread on crisp toast to make a delicious appetizer or accompaniment to meat or vegetable dishes.

INGREDIENTS

2 whole garlic heads
extra virgin olive oil
fresh rosemary sprigs
loaf of ciabatta or thick baguette
chopped fresh rosemary
salt and freshly ground black
pepper

SERVES 4

1 Slice the tops from the heads of garlic using a sharp kitchen knife.

2 Brush the garlic heads with extra virgin olive oil and add a few sprigs of fresh rosemary before wrapping in foil. Cook the foil parcels on a medium-hot grill for 25–30 minutes, turning occasionally, until the garlic is soft.

3 Slice the bread and brush each slice generously with olive oil. Toast the slices on the grill until crisp and golden, turning once.

4 Squeeze the garlic cloves from their skins onto the toasts. Sprinkle with the chopped fresh rosemary and olive oil, and add salt and black pepper to taste.

ROASTED PEPPER ANTIPASTO

• • •

Jars of Italian mixed peppers in olive oil are a common sight in supermarkets, yet none can compete with this freshly made version, perfect as an appetizer or served with cold cuts.

INGREDIENTS
3 red bell peppers
2 yellow or orange bell peppers
2 green bell peppers
1/2 cup sun-dried tomatoes in oil,
drained
1 garlic clove
2 tablespoons balsamic vinegar
5 tablespoons olive oil
few drops of chili sauce
4 canned artichoke hearts, drained
and sliced
salt and freshly ground black
pepper
fresh basil leaves, to garnish

SERVES 6

1 Cook the whole peppers on a medium-hot grill, turning frequently, for 10–15 minutes, until they begin to char. Cover the grilled peppers with a clean dish towel and allow them to cool for 5 minutes.

2 Use a sharp kitchen knife to slice the sun-dried tomatoes into thin strips. Thinly slice the garlic clove.

3 Whisk together the balsamic vinegar, olive oil and chili sauce in a small bowl, then season with a little salt and freshly ground black pepper.

4 Cut off the stalks and slice the peppers. Mix with the artichokes, sun-dried tomatoes and garlic. Add the dressing and sprinkle with basil leaves.

HERB-STUFFED MINI-VEGETABLES

• • •

These little hors d'oeuvres are ideal for parties, as they can be prepared in advance and simply assembled and cooked at the last minute.

INGREDIENTS

30 mini-vegetables: zucchini, pattypan squash and large button mushrooms
2 tablespoons olive oil
fresh basil or parsley, to garnish

FOR THE STUFFING
2 tablespoons olive oil
1 onion, finely chopped
1 garlic clove, finely chopped
4 ounces button mushrooms, finely chopped
1 zucchini, finely chopped
1 red bell pepper, finely chopped
1/3 cup orzo pasta or long-grain rice
1/3 cup tomato sauce
1/2 teaspoon dried thyme
1/2 cup chicken stock
1–2 teaspoons chopped fresh basil or parsley
2 ounces mozzarella or fontina cheese, coarsely grated
salt and freshly ground black pepper

MAKES 30

1 For the stuffing, heat the oil in a pan over medium heat. Add the onion and cook for 2 minutes, until tender. Stir in the garlic, mushrooms, zucchini and red pepper. Season and cook for 2 minutes, until the vegetables soften.

2 Stir in the pasta or rice, the tomato sauce, thyme and stock and bring to a boil, stirring. Reduce the heat and simmer for 10–12 minutes, until reduced and thickened. Remove from the heat and let cool slightly. Stir in the basil or parsley and the cheese.

3 Drop the zucchini and squash into boiling water and cook for 3 minutes. Drain and refresh under cold running water. Trim the bottoms so they are flat, trim a small slice off the tops and scoop out the centers with a spoon or melon baller. Remove the stems from the mushrooms. Brush all of the vegetables with olive oil.

4 Using a teaspoon, fill the vegetables with the stuffing and arrange on a rack. Cook on a medium-hot grill or broil for 10–15 minutes, until the filling is hot and bubbling. Garnish with fresh basil or parsley. The vegetables can be served either warm or at room temperature.

POLPETTE WITH MOZZARELLA AND TOMATO

° ° °

*These Italian-style meatballs are made with beef and topped with creamy melted
mozzarella and savory anchovies.*

INGREDIENTS
*½ slice white bread, crusts
removed
3 tablespoons milk
1½ pounds ground beef
1 egg, beaten
⅔ cup dry bread crumbs
olive oil for brushing
2 beefsteak or other large
tomatoes, sliced
1 tablespoon chopped fresh
oregano
6 slices mozzarella cheese
6 canned anchovy fillets, drained
and cut in half lengthwise
salt and freshly ground black
pepper*
SERVES 6

1 Put the bread and milk into a small
saucepan and heat very gently, until the
bread absorbs all the milk. Mash it to a
pulp and set aside to cool.

2 Put the ground beef into a bowl
with the bread mixture and the egg and
season with plenty of salt and freshly
ground black pepper. Mix well, then
shape the mixture into 6 patties, using
your hands. Sprinkle the bread crumbs
onto a plate and dredge the patties,
coating them thoroughly.

3 Brush the polpette with olive
oil and cook them on a hot grill for
2–3 minutes on one side, until brown.
Turn them over.

4 Without removing the polpette
from the grill, lay a slice of tomato on
top of each one, sprinkle with chopped
oregano and season with salt and
pepper. Place a mozzarella slice on top
and arrange 2 strips of anchovy in a
cross over the cheese.

5 Cook for another 4–5 minutes,
until the polpette are cooked through
and the mozzarella has melted.

STUFFED KIBBEH

. . .

*Kibbeh is a tasty Middle Eastern speciality of ground lamb and bulgur, which can be
eaten raw or shaped into patties and cooked on the grill.*

INGREDIENTS

1 pound lean lamb
3 tablespoons olive oil
avocado slices and fresh cilantro
sprigs, to serve

FOR THE KIBBEH
1 1/3 cups bulgur
1 fresh red chili, seeded and
roughly chopped
1 onion, roughly chopped
salt and freshly ground black
pepper

FOR THE STUFFING
1 onion, finely chopped
2/3 cup pine nuts
2 tablespoons olive oil
1 1/2 teaspoons ground allspice
4 tablespoons chopped fresh
cilantro

SERVES 4–6

1 Roughly cut the lamb into chunks,
using a heavy kitchen knife. Process the
chunks in a blender or food processor
until finely ground. Divide the ground
meat into two equal portions and set
aside until needed.

2 To make the kibbeh, soak the
bulgur in cold water for 15 minutes.
Drain well, then process in the blender
or food processor with the chopped
chili and onion, half the meat and
plenty of salt and pepper.

3 To make the stuffing, fry the
onion and pine nuts in the olive oil
for 5 minutes. Add the allspice and
remaining ground meat and fry gently,
breaking up the meat with a wooden
spoon, until browned. Stir in the
cilantro and a little seasoning.

4 Turn the kibbeh mixture out onto
a clean work surface and use your
hands to shape the mixture into a flat
round. Divide into 12 wedges.

5 Flatten a wedge in the palm of your
hand and spoon a little stuffing onto
the center. Bring the edges of the kibbeh
over the stuffing to enclose it. Form
into a firm egg-shaped mold between
the palms of your hands, making sure
that the filling is completely enclosed.
Repeat with the other wedges.

6 To grill the kibbeh, lightly brush
with olive oil and cook on a medium
grill for 10–15 minutes, turning
carefully, until evenly browned and
cooked through. To fry the kibbeh,
heat oil to a depth of 2 inches in a large
pan until a few kibbeh crumbs sizzle
when dropped on the surface. Lower
half the kibbeh into the oil and fry for
about 5 minutes, until golden. Drain on
paper towels and keep hot while frying
the remainder. Serve hot with avocado
slices and fresh cilantro sprigs.

HERB POLENTA

∘ ∘ ∘

Golden polenta made with fresh summer herbs and served with grilled tomatoes makes a tasty appetizer or light snack.

INGREDIENTS

3 cups stock or water
1 teaspoon salt
1 cup polenta
2 tablespoons butter
5 tablespoons mixed chopped fresh parsley, chives and basil, plus extra to garnish
olive oil for brushing
4 large plum or beef tomatoes, halved
salt and freshly ground black pepper

SERVES 4

3 Remove from the heat and stir in the butter, chopped herbs and pepper.

4 Lightly grease a wide pan or dish and pour the polenta into it, spreading it evenly. Set aside until cool and set.

1 Prepare the polenta in advance: Place the stock or water in a saucepan, with the salt, and bring to a boil. Reduce the heat and stir in the polenta.

2 Stir constantly over moderate heat for 5 minutes, until the polenta begins to thicken and come away from the sides of the saucepan.

5 Turn out the polenta and cut into squares or stamp out rounds with a large cookie cutter. Brush with olive oil. Lightly brush the tomatoes with oil and sprinkle with salt and pepper. Cook the tomatoes and polenta on a medium-hot grill for about 5 minutes, turning once. Serve garnished with fresh herbs.

Cook's Tip

Try using fresh basil or fresh chives alone, for a distinctive flavor.

BRIE PARCELS WITH ALMONDS

• • •

*Creamy French Brie makes a sophisticated appetizer or light meal, wrapped in
grape leaves and served hot with chunks of crusty bread.*

2 Cut the Brie into four chunks and
place each chunk on a grape leaf.

3 Mix together the chives, ground
almonds, peppercorns and olive oil, and
place a spoonful on top of each piece of
cheese. Sprinkle with sliced almonds.

4 Fold the grape leaves over tightly
to enclose the cheese completely.
Brush the parcels with olive oil and
cook on a hot grill for 3–4 minutes,
until the cheese is hot and melting.
Serve immediately.

INGREDIENTS

*4 large grape leaves, in brine
7-ounce piece Brie cheese
2 tablespoons chopped fresh chives
2 tablespoons ground almonds
1 teaspoon crushed black
peppercorns
1 tablespoon olive oil, plus extra
for brushing
sliced almonds*

SERVES 4

1 Rinse the grape leaves thoroughly
under cold running water and dry them
well. Spread the leaves out on a clean
work surface or chopping board.

TOFU STEAKS

• • •

Vegetarians and meat-eaters alike will enjoy these barbecued tofu steaks. The combination of ingredients in the marinade gives the steaks a distinctly Japanese flavor.

INGREDIENTS

1 container fresh tofu (4 × 3¹/₄ × 1¹/₄ inches), 11 ounces drained weight
2 scallions, thinly sliced, to garnish
mixed salad leaves, to garnish

FOR THE MARINADE
3 tablespoons sake
2 tablespoons soy sauce
1 teaspoon sesame oil
1 garlic clove, crushed
1 tablespoon grated fresh ginger
1 scallion, finely chopped

SERVES 4

1 Wrap the tofu in a clean dish towel and place it on a chopping board. Put a large plate on top and let stand for 30 minutes to remove any excess water.

2 Slice the tofu horizontally into three pieces, then cut the slices into quarters. Set aside. Mix the ingredients for the marinade in a large bowl. Add the tofu to the bowl in a single layer and allow to marinate for 30 minutes. Drain the tofu steaks and reserve the marinade to use for basting.

3 Cook the steaks on the grill for 3 minutes on each side, basting regularly with the marinade, or fry them for 3 minutes in a large pan.

4 Arrange 3 tofu steaks on each plate. Any remaining marinade can be heated in a pan and then poured over the steaks. Sprinkle with the scallions and garnish with mixed salad leaves. Serve immediately.

Cook's Tip
Tofu is easily obtainable from supermarkets and health food stores, and is an ideal alternative to meat.

GRILLED ASPARAGUS WITH SALT-CURED HAM

• • •

Grilled asparagus has a wonderfully intense flavor that stands up well to the wrapping of crisp, salty ham. Serve this traditional tapas dish with drinks before a meal.

INGREDIENTS

6 slices of Serrano ham
12 asparagus spears
1 tablespoon olive oil
sea salt and coarsely ground black
pepper

SERVES 4

1 Halve each slice of ham lengthwise and wrap one half around each of the asparagus spears.

2 Brush the ham and asparagus lightly with olive oil and sprinkle with salt and pepper. Cook on a medium grill for about 4 minutes, turning frequently, until the asparagus is tender but still firm. Serve at once.

Cook's Tip
If you can't find Serrano ham, try using Italian prosciutto or Portuguese presunto.

POTATO SKINS WITH CAJUN DIP

∘ ∘ ∘

As an alternative to deep-frying, grilling potato skins crisps them up in no time and gives them a wonderful charbroiled flavor. This spicy dip makes the perfect partner.

INGREDIENTS

4 large baking potatoes
olive oil for brushing
1 cup plain yogurt
2 garlic cloves, crushed
2 teaspoons tomato paste
1 teaspoon green chili paste or
1 small green chili, chopped
½ teaspoon celery salt
salt and freshly ground black
pepper

SERVES 4

1 Bake or microwave the potatoes until tender. Cut them in half and scoop out the flesh, leaving a thin layer of flesh on the skins. The scooped-out potato can be reserved in the refrigerator or freezer for another meal.

2 Cut each potato shell in half again and lightly brush the skins with olive oil. Cook on a medium-hot grill for 4–5 minutes, or until crisp.

3 To make the dip, mix together the remaining ingredients in a bowl. Serve the potato skins with the Cajun dip on the side.

Cook's Tip
If you don't have any chili paste or fresh chilies, add one or two drops of hot pepper sauce to the dip instead.

SPICY CHICKEN WINGS

• • •

These deliciously sticky bites will appeal to adults and children alike, although younger eaters might prefer a little less chili powder.

INGREDIENTS

8 plump chicken wings
2 large garlic cloves, cut
into slivers
1 tablespoon olive oil
1 tablespoon paprika
1 teaspoon chili powder
1 teaspoon dried oregano
salt and freshly ground black
pepper
lime wedges, to serve

SERVES 4

1 Using a small, sharp kitchen knife, make one or two cuts in the skin of each chicken wing and slide a sliver of garlic under the skin. Brush the wings generously with the olive oil.

2 In a large bowl, stir together the paprika, chili powder and oregano and season with plenty of salt and pepper. Add the chicken wings and toss together until very lightly coated in the mixture.

3 Cook the chicken wings on a medium grill for 15 minutes, until they are cooked through and the skins are blackened and crisp. Serve with fresh lime wedges.

CHICKEN WINGS TERIYAKI STYLE

° ° °

This Japanese-style glaze is very simple to prepare and adds a unique flavor to the meat.
The glaze can be used with any cut of chicken or with fish.

INGREDIENTS

1 garlic clove, crushed
3 tablespoons soy sauce
2 tablespoons dry sherry
2 teaspoons honey
2 teaspoons grated fresh ginger
1 teaspoon sesame oil
12 chicken wings
1 tablespoon sesame seeds, toasted

SERVES 4

1 Place the garlic, soy sauce, sherry, honey, grated ginger and sesame oil in a large bowl and beat with a fork, to mix the ingredients together evenly.

2 Add the chicken wings and toss thoroughly, to coat in the marinade. Cover the bowl with plastic wrap and chill for 30 minutes or longer.

3 Cook the chicken wings on a fairly hot grill for 20–25 minutes, turning occasionally and basting with the remaining marinade.

4 Sprinkle the chicken wings with sesame seeds. Serve the wings on their own as an appetizer or side dish, or as a light meal with a crisp green salad.

SKEWERED LAMB WITH RED ONION SALSA

A simple salsa makes a refreshing accompaniment to this summery dish—make sure you use a mild-flavored red onion that is fresh and crisp, and a tomato that is ripe and full of flavor.

INGREDIENTS

8 ounces lean lamb, cubed
1/2 teaspoon ground cumin
1 teaspoon ground paprika
1 tablespoon olive oil
salt and freshly ground black
pepper

FOR THE SALSA

1 red onion, very thinly sliced
1 large tomato, seeded and
chopped
1 tablespoon red wine vinegar
3 or 4 fresh basil or mint leaves,
roughly torn
small mint leaves, to garnish

SERVES 4

1 Place the lamb in a large bowl with the cumin, paprika and olive oil and season with plenty of salt and freshly ground black pepper. Toss well. Cover the bowl with plastic wrap and let sit in a cool place for several hours or in the refrigerator overnight, so that the lamb fully absorbs the spicy flavors.

2 Spear the lamb cubes on four small skewers. If using wooden skewers, soak them first in cold water for at least 30 minutes to prevent them from burning when placed on the grill.

3 To make the salsa, put the sliced onion, tomato, red wine vinegar and torn fresh basil or mint leaves in a small bowl and stir together until thoroughly blended. Season to taste with salt and garnish with mint.

4 Cook the skewered lamb on a hot grill or under a hot broiler for 5–10 minutes, turning the skewers frequently, until the lamb is well browned but still slightly pink in the center. Serve hot, with the salsa.

SPICY MEATBALLS

◦ ◦ ◦

These meatballs are delicious served piping hot with chili sauce. Keep the sauce on the side so that everyone can add as much heat as they like.

2 Add the ground beef, shallots, garlic, bread crumbs, beaten egg and parsley, with plenty of salt and pepper. Mix well, then use your hands to shape the mixture into 18 small balls.

3 Brush the meatballs with olive oil and cook on a medium grill, or fry them in a large pan, for about 10–15 minutes, turning regularly until evenly browned and cooked through.

INGREDIENTS

4 ounces fresh spicy sausages
4 ounces ground beef
2 shallots, finely chopped
2 garlic cloves, finely chopped
1½ cups fresh white bread crumbs
1 egg, beaten
2 tablespoons chopped fresh parsley, plus extra to garnish
1 tablespoon olive oil
salt and freshly ground black pepper
Tabasco or other hot chili sauce, to serve

SERVES 6

1 Use your hands to remove the skins from the sausages, placing the sausage meat in a mixing bowl and breaking it up with a fork.

4 Transfer the meatballs to a warm dish and sprinkle with chopped fresh parsley. Serve with chili sauce.

FIVE-SPICE RIB-STICKERS

· · ·

To make these a real success, choose the meatiest spareribs you can find;
remember to keep a supply of paper napkins within easy reach.

2 Mix together all the remaining ingredients except the scallions; pour this mixture over the ribs. Toss well to coat evenly. Cover the bowl and let marinate in the refrigerator overnight.

3 Cook the ribs on a medium-hot grill, turning frequently, for 30–40 minutes. Brush occasionally with the remaining marinade.

INGREDIENTS

2¼ pounds Chinese-style pork
spareribs
2 teaspoons Chinese five-spice
powder
2 garlic cloves, crushed
1 tablespoon grated fresh ginger
½ teaspoon chili sauce
4 tablespoons dark soy sauce
3 tablespoons dark brown sugar
1 tablespoon sunflower oil
4 scallions

SERVES 4

1 If the spareribs are still attached to each other, cut between them to separate them (or you could ask your butcher to do this when you buy them). Place the spareribs in a large bowl.

4 While the ribs are cooking, finely slice the scallions. Sprinkle them over the ribs and serve immediately.

SALMON WITH SPICY PESTO

· · ·

This is a great way to bone salmon steaks to give a solid piece of fish. The pesto is made with sunflower or pumpkin seeds and chilies rather than the classic basil and pine nuts.

INGREDIENTS

4 salmon steaks, about
8 ounces each
2 tablespoons sunflower oil
finely grated rind and juice
of 1 lime
salt and freshly ground
black pepper

FOR THE PESTO
6 mild fresh red chilies
2 garlic cloves
2 tablespoons sunflower or
pumpkin seeds
juice and finely grated rind
of 1 lime
5 tablespoons olive oil

SERVES 4

1 Insert a very sharp knife close to the top of the bone. Working close to the bone, cut your way to the end of the steak to release one side. Repeat with the other side. Pull out any visible extra bones with a pair of tweezers.

2 Sprinkle salt on a work surface and take hold of the end of the salmon piece, skin side down. Insert the knife between the skin and the flesh and, working away from you, remove the skin, keeping the knife as close to it as possible. Repeat for each piece of fish.

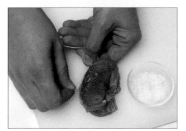

3 Curl each piece of fish into a round, with the thinner end wrapped around the fatter end. Secure the shape tightly with a length of string.

4 Rub the sunflower oil into the boneless fish rounds. Put the salmon in a large bowl or dish and add the lime juice and rind and the salt and pepper. Allow the salmon to marinate in the refrigerator for up to 2 hours.

5 For the pesto, seed the chilies and place, with the garlic cloves, sunflower or pumpkin seeds, lime juice, rind and seasoning, in a food processor. Process until well mixed. With the blades moving, gradually pour in the olive oil until the sauce has thickened and emulsified. Drain the salmon from its marinade. Cook the fish steaks on a medium grill for 5 minutes on each side and serve with the spicy pesto.

GRILLED JUMBO SHRIMP WITH ROMESCO SAUCE

*This sauce comes from the Catalan region of Spain and is served with fish and seafood.
Its main ingredients are pimiento, tomatoes, garlic and almonds.*

INGREDIENTS

24 uncooked jumbo shrimp
2–3 tablespoons olive oil
flat-leaf parsley, to garnish
lemon wedges, to serve

FOR THE SAUCE

2 ripe, flavorful tomatoes
4 tablespoons olive oil
1 onion, chopped
4 garlic cloves, chopped
1 canned pimiento, chopped
1/2 teaspoons crushed red pepper or
chili powder
5 tablespoons fish stock
2 tablespoons white wine
10 blanched almonds
1 tablespoon red wine vinegar
salt

SERVES 4

1 To make the sauce, immerse the tomatoes in boiling water for about 30 seconds, then refresh them under cold running water. Peel away the skins and roughly chop the flesh.

2 Heat 2 tablespoons of the oil. Add the onion and 3 of the garlic cloves; cook until soft. Add the pimiento, tomatoes, crushed red pepper, fish stock and wine. Cover and simmer for 30 minutes.

3 Toast the almonds under the broiler until golden. Transfer to a blender or food processor and grind coarsely. Add the remaining 2 tablespoons oil, the vinegar and the last garlic clove and process until evenly combined. Add the tomato and pimiento sauce and process until smooth. Season with salt.

4 Remove the heads from the shrimp, leaving them otherwise unshelled, and, with a sharp knife, slit each one down the back and remove the dark vein. Rinse and pat dry on paper towels. Toss the shrimp in olive oil, then spread them out on the grill and cook over medium heat for 2–3 minutes on each side, until pink. Serve at once, garnished with parsley and accompanied by lemon wedges and the romesco sauce.

GRILLED MUSSELS WITH PARSLEY AND PARMESAN

• • •

*Mussels release an irresistible aroma as they cook on the grill. Don't be surprised
if they are devoured the moment they are ready.*

INGREDIENTS

1 pound fresh mussels
3 tablespoons water
1 tablespoon melted butter
1 tablespoon olive oil
3 tablespoons freshly grated
Parmesan cheese
2 tablespoons chopped fresh parsley
2 garlic cloves, finely chopped
½ teaspoon ground black pepper
crusty French bread, to serve

SERVES 4

2 Place the mussels with the water in a large saucepan. Cover and steam for 5 minutes, or until all of the mussels have opened.

4 In a large bowl, mix together the melted butter, olive oil, grated Parmesan cheese, chopped parsley, garlic and ground black pepper.

1 Scrub the mussels, scraping off any barnacles and pulling out the beards. Tap any closed mussels sharply with a knife and discard any that fail to open.

3 Drain the mussels, discarding any that remain closed. Snap the top shell off of each, leaving the mussel still attached to the bottom shell.

5 Using a spoon, place a small amount of the cheese mixture on top of each mussel.

6 Cook the mussels in a saucepan on a medium grill for 2–3 minutes, or until the mussels are sizzling hot. Serve immediately, with crusty French bread.

QUICK SEAFOOD PIZZA

• • •

Make four mini-pizzas or one large one with the same quantities of ingredients.
If you are short of time, use a pizza-crust mix instead of making the dough.

INGREDIENTS

FOR THE PIZZA CRUST
1 teaspoon active dry yeast
4 cups bread flour
1 tablespoon sugar
1 teaspoon sea salt
1¼ cups lukewarm water
2 tablespoons extra virgin olive oil

FOR THE FISH TOPPING
1 tablespoon olive oil
1 onion, finely chopped
1¾ pound canned or fresh plum
tomatoes, chopped
salt and freshly ground black
pepper
1 tablespoon chopped fresh thyme
4 ounces cherry tomatoes, halved
12 fresh anchovy fillets, or 1 can
anchovy fillets, drained
8 fresh, peeled shrimp
a few sprigs of fresh thyme,
to garnish

SERVES 4

1 Stir the yeast into the flour in a large bowl. Add the sugar and sea salt and mix together well.

2 Add the water and olive oil to the bowl, and stir to make a firm dough.

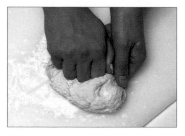

3 Knead the dough for about 10 minutes. Cover and let sit in a warm place until it has doubled in size.

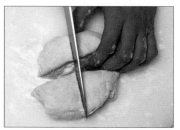

4 Knock back the dough and knead for 5 minutes, then cut the dough into 4 pieces. Shape each of the 4 pieces of dough into a 5-inch round.

5 Fry the onions until soft. Add the tomatoes, seasoning and thyme and simmer for 15 minutes. Brush the pizza dough rounds with olive oil and cook on a medium-hot grill, oiled side down, for 6–8 minutes, until firm and golden underneath. Oil the uncooked side and turn the pizzas over.

6 Cut the cherry tomatoes in half. On each of the pizzas place a spoonful of the sauce, three anchovy fillets, two shrimp and some cherry tomato halves. Return the pizzas to the grill and cook for another 8–10 minutes, until golden and crispy. Sprinkle a few fresh sprigs of thyme on top of the pizzas to serve.

Variation

Add your favorite seafood, such as fresh or canned mussels, to the topping.

CIABATTA WITH MOZZARELLA AND ONIONS

• • •

*Ciabatta, a crusty, flavorful Italian bread, is even more delicious when made with spinach,
sun-dried tomatoes or olives: You can find these variations in many supermarkets.*

INGREDIENTS
1 loaf of ciabatta
4 tablespoons red pesto
2 small onions
olive oil, for brushing
8 ounces mozzarella cheese, sliced
8 black olives, halved and pitted

MAKES 4

1 Cut the bread in half horizontally
and toast the cut sides lightly on the
grill. Spread with the pesto.

2 Peel the onions and cut them
horizontally into slices. Brush with
oil and cook on a hot grill for
4–5 minutes, until caramelized.

3 Arrange the cheese slices on the
bread. Add the onion slices and scatter
some olives on top. Cut in half. Return
to the grill or broiler to melt the cheese.

CROSTINI WITH TOMATO AND ANCHOVY

• • •

Crostini are little rounds of bread cut from a baguette and crisply toasted,
then covered with a topping, such as this savory mixture of tomato and anchovy.

2 Cut the bread diagonally into 8 slices about ½-inch thick and brush with the remaining oil. Toast on the grill until golden, turning once.

3 Spoon a little of the tomato mixture onto each slice of bread. Place an anchovy fillet on each one and dot with the halved olives. Serve the crostini garnished with sprigs of fresh basil.

INGREDIENTS

4 tablespoons olive oil
2 garlic cloves
4 tomatoes, peeled and chopped
1 tablespoon chopped fresh basil
1 tablespoon tomato paste
1 small baguette (large enough to give 8 slices)
8 canned anchovy fillets
12 black olives, halved and pitted
salt and freshly ground black pepper
fresh basil, to garnish

MAKES 8

1 Heat half the olive oil in a frying pan and fry the whole garlic cloves with the chopped tomatoes for about 4 minutes. Stir in the chopped basil and tomato paste and season with plenty of salt and freshly ground black pepper.

Variation

CROSTINI WITH ONION AND OLIVE
Fry 2 large onions, sliced, in 2 tablespoons olive oil until golden. Stir in 8 chopped anchovy fillets, 12 halved, pitted black olives, some seasoning, and 1 teaspoon dried thyme. Spread the bread with 1 tablespoon black olive paste and cover with the onion mixture.

Meat
Dishes

———✦———

Succulent cuts of meat are often the starting-point when planning

a meal cooked on the grill, and charbroiling gives meat a unique flavor.

A perfect steak or lamb chop, simply seasoned and brushed with oil

before broiling, is utterly delicious. Even ordinary sausages and burgers

for an impromptu family supper can be turned into a treat on the grill.

With a little forethought you can add variety and originality to your

cooking by marinating the meat for a few hours before you cook it.

The simplest marinade will work wonders: improving the texture and

juiciness of the meat as well as adding the flavors of herbs and spices.

The recipes in this chapter draw on cuisines from all over the world to

offer an exciting range of dishes that are all easy to prepare and delicious.

MIXED GRILL SKEWERS WITH HORSERADISH SAUCE

• • •

This hearty selection of meats, cooked on a skewer and drizzled with horseradish sauce, makes a popular main course. Keep all the pieces of meat about the same thickness so they cook evenly.

INGREDIENTS

4 small lamb noisettes, each about 1 inch thick
4 lamb kidneys
4 slices lean bacon
8 cherry tomatoes
8 chipolata sausages
12–16 bay leaves
salt and freshly ground black pepper

FOR THE HORSERADISH SAUCE
2 tablespoons horseradish relish
3 tablespoons melted butter

SERVES 4

3 Thread the lamb noisettes, bacon-wrapped kidneys and cherry tomatoes, chipolatas and bay leaves onto 4 long metal skewers. Set aside while you prepare the sauce.

4 Mix the horseradish relish with the melted butter in a small bowl and stir until thoroughly mixed.

5 Brush a little of the horseradish sauce over the meat and sprinkle with salt and freshly ground black pepper.

6 Cook the skewers on a medium grill for 12 minutes, turning them occasionally, until the meat is golden brown and thoroughly cooked. Serve hot, drizzled with the remaining sauce.

1 Trim any excess fat from the lamb noisettes with a sharp knife. Halve the kidneys and remove the cores, using kitchen scissors.

2 Cut each bacon slice in half and wrap around the tomatoes and kidneys.

SAUSAGES WITH PRUNES AND BACON

○ ○ ○

*Sausages are a perennial barbecue favorite, and this is a delicious and
unusual way to prepare them. Serve with crusty French bread or warmed ciabatta.*

2 Spread the cut surface with the
mustard and then place 3 prunes in
each sausage, pressing them in firmly.

3 Stretch the bacon slices out thinly,
using the back of a metal spatula.

4 Wrap one bacon slice tightly
around each of the sausages, to
hold them in shape. Cook over a hot
grill for 15–18 minutes, turning
occasionally, until evenly browned and
thoroughly cooked. Serve at once, with
lots of fresh crusty bread and mustard.

INGREDIENTS

*8 large garlic and herb pork
sausages, or other good-quality
meaty sausages
2 tablespoons Dijon mustard,
plus extra to serve
24 pitted prunes
8 slices lean smoked bacon*

SERVES 4

1 Use a sharp knife to cut a long slit
down the length of each sausage, about
three-quarters of the way through.

SHISH KEBAB

• • •

Many different kinds of kebab are eaten throughout the Middle East, and they are almost always cooked over an open wood or charcoal fire.

INGREDIENTS
1 pound boned leg of lamb, cubed
1 large green bell pepper, seeded
and cut into squares
1 large yellow bell pepper, seeded
and cut into squares
8 baby onions, halved
8 ounces button mushrooms
4 tomatoes, halved
1 tablespoons melted butter
bulgur, to serve

FOR THE MARINADE
3 tablespoons olive oil
juice of 1 lemon
2 garlic cloves, crushed
1 large onion, grated
1 tablespoon fresh oregano
salt and freshly ground black
pepper

SERVES 4

1 First make the marinade: Blend together the olive oil, lemon juice, crushed garlic, onion, fresh oregano and seasoning. Place the meat in a shallow dish and pour the marinade over it. Cover with plastic wrap and allow to marinate for several hours, or overnight, in the refrigerator.

2 Thread the lamb onto metal skewers, alternating with pieces of pepper, onions and mushrooms. Thread the tomatoes onto separate skewers.

3 Cook the kebabs and tomatoes on a hot grill for 10 minutes, turning occasionally and basting with butter. Serve with prepared bulgur.

BACON KOFTA KEBABS AND SALAD

• • •

*Kofta kebabs can be made with any type of ground meat, but bacon is very successful,
if you have a food processor.*

INGREDIENTS

9 ounces lean bacon slices,
roughly chopped
1 small onion, roughly chopped
1 celery stick, roughly chopped
5 tablespoons fresh whole-wheat
bread crumbs
3 tablespoons chopped fresh thyme
2 tablespoons Worcestershire sauce
1 egg, beaten
salt and freshly ground black
pepper
olive oil, for brushing

FOR THE SALAD
3/4 cup bulgur wheat
4 tablespoons toasted sunflower
seeds
1 tablespoon olive oil
salt and freshly ground black
pepper
handful of celery leaves, chopped

SERVES 4

1 Place the bacon, onion, celery and bread crumbs in a food processor and process until chopped. Add the thyme, Worcestershire sauce and seasoning. Bind to a firm mixture with the egg.

2 Divide the mixture into 8 equal portions and use your hands to shape them around 8 bamboo skewers.

3 For the salad, place the bulgur in a bowl and pour boiling water over it to cover. Let stand for 30 minutes, until the grains are tender.

4 Drain well, then stir in the sunflower seeds, olive oil, salt and pepper. Stir in the celery leaves.

5 Cook the kofta skewers over a medium-hot grill for 8–10 minutes, turning occasionally, until golden brown. Serve with the salad.

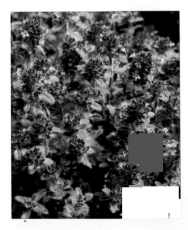

PEPPERED STEAKS IN BEER AND GARLIC

· · ·

The robust flavors of this dish will satisfy the heartiest appetites.
Serve the steaks with baked potatoes and a crisp mixed salad.

2 Remove the steaks from the dish and reserve the marinade. Sprinkle the peppercorns over the steaks, and press them into the surface.

3 Cook the steaks on a hot grill, basting them occasionally with the reserved marinade during cooking. (Take care when basting, as the alcohol will tend to flare up: Spoon or brush on just a small amount at a time.)

INGREDIENTS

4 beef sirloin or round steaks,
about 6 ounces each
2 garlic cloves, crushed
1/2 cup brown ale or stout
2 tablespoons dark brown sugar
2 tablespoons Worcestershire sauce
1 tablespoon corn oil
1 tablespoon crushed black
peppercorns

SERVES 4

1 Place the steaks in a dish and add the garlic, ale or stout, sugar, Worcestershire sauce and oil. Turn to coat evenly, then let marinate in the refrigerator for 2–3 hours or overnight.

4 Turn the steaks once during cooking, and cook them for about 3–6 minutes on each side, depending on how rare you like them.

SIRLOIN STEAKS WITH BLOODY MARY SAUCE

• • •

This cocktail of ingredients is just as delicious as the drink that inspired it, and since the alcohol evaporates in cooking, it is perfectly safe to serve to children.

INGREDIENTS

4 sirloin steaks, about
8 ounces each

FOR THE MARINADE
2 tablespoons dark soy sauce
4 tablespoons balsamic vinegar
2 tablespoons olive oil

FOR THE BLOODY MARY SAUCE
2¼ pounds very ripe tomatoes,
peeled and chopped
tomato paste, if required
½ cup chopped onions
2 scallions
1 teaspoon chopped fresh cilantro
1 teaspoon ground cumin
1 teaspoon salt
1 tablespoon fresh lime juice
½ cup beef consommé
¼ cup vodka
1 tablespoon Worcestershire sauce

SERVES 4

1 Lay the steaks in a shallow dish. Mix the marinade ingredients together, pour over the steaks and let marinate in the refrigerator for at least 2 hours, turning once or twice.

2 Place all the sauce ingredients in a food processor and blend to a fairly smooth texture. If the tomatoes are not quite ripe, add a little tomato paste. Put in a saucepan, bring to a boil and simmer for about 5 minutes.

3 Remove the steaks from the dish and discard the marinade. Cook the steaks on a medium-hot grill for about 3–6 minutes on each side, depending on how rare you like them, turning once during cooking. Serve the steaks with the Bloody Mary Sauce.

BEEF RIB WITH ONION SAUCE

• • •

*Rib of beef is a classic large cut for roasting, but just one rib, grilled on the bone, and then
carved into succulent slices, makes a perfect dish for two. Serve with a mellow red onion sauce.*

INGREDIENTS

*1 beef rib on the bone, about 2¼
pounds and about 1½ inches
thick, well trimmed of fat
1 teaspoon "steak pepper" or
lightly crushed black peppercorns
1 tablespoon coarse sea salt,
crushed
2–3 tablespoons olive oil*

FOR THE RED ONION SAUCE
*3 tablespoons butter
1 large red onion or 8–10 shallots,
sliced
1 cup beef or chicken stock
1–2 tablespoons red currant jelly
¼ teaspoon dried thyme
salt and freshly ground black
pepper*

SERVES 2

1 Wipe the beef with damp paper
towels. Mix the steak pepper or
crushed peppercorns with the crushed
salt and press onto both sides of the
meat. Let the meat stand, loosely
covered, for 30 minutes.

2 To make the sauce, melt the butter
over medium heat. Add the onion
or shallots and cook for 3 minutes,
until softened. Add the wine, stock,
jelly and thyme and bring to a boil.
Reduce the heat and simmer for
30–35 minutes, until the liquid has
evaporated and the sauce has
thickened. Season and keep warm.

3 Brush the meat with olive oil and
cook on a hot grill, or in a pan over
high heat, for 5–8 minutes on each
side, depending on how rare you like it.
Transfer the beef to a board, cover
loosely and let stand for about 10
minutes. Using a knife, loosen the meat
from the rib bone, then carve into thick
slices. Serve with the onion sauce.

STILTON BURGERS
. . .

A variation on the traditional hamburger, this tasty recipe contains a delicious surprise:
a creamy filling of lightly melted Stilton cheese.

INGREDIENTS

1 pound ground beef
1 onion, chopped
1 celery stick, chopped
1 teaspoon dried mixed herbs
1 teaspoon prepared mustard
¹/₂ cup crumbled Stilton cheese
4 hamburger buns
salt and freshly ground black
pepper
salad and mustard pickle, to serve

SERVES 4

1 Mix the ground beef with the chopped onion, celery, mixed herbs and mustard. Season well with salt and pepper, and bring together with your hands to form a firm mixture.

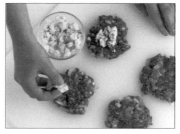

2 Divide the mixture into 8 equal portions. Shape 4 portions into rounds and flatten each one slightly. Place a little of the crumbled cheese in the center of each round.

3 Shape and flatten the remaining four portions and place on top. Use your hands to mold the rounds together, encasing the crumbled cheese and shaping them into four burgers.

4 Cook on a medium grill for about 10 minutes or until cooked through, turning once. Split the hamburger buns and place a burger inside each one. Serve with salad and mustard pickle.

THAI BEEF SALAD

• • •

A hearty salad of beef and crunchy vegetables, laced with a tangy chili and lime dressing. The grilled meat gives the salad a truly delicious flavor.

INGREDIENTS

*2 sirloin steaks, about
8 ounces each
1 red onion, finely sliced
½ cucumber, sliced into matchsticks
1 stalk lemongrass, finely chopped
2 tablespoons chopped scallions
juice of 2 limes
1–2 tablespoons Thai fish sauce
2–4 red chilies, finely sliced, to
garnish
fresh cilantro, Chinese mustard
cabbage and mint leaves, to
garnish*

SERVES 4

1 Grill or pan-fry the beef steaks until they are medium rare. Allow the steaks to rest for 10–15 minutes.

2 When the steaks have cooled slightly, slice them thinly, using a heavy knife, and put the slices into a large bowl.

3 Add the sliced onion, cucumber matchsticks and chopped lemongrass.

4 Add the scallions. Toss and season with lime juice and Thai fish sauce. Serve at room temperature or chilled, garnished with the chilies, cilantro, mustard cabbage and mint.

NEW ORLEANS STEAK SALAD

. . .

The New Orleans "poor boy" started life in the Creole community, as a sandwich filled with leftover scraps. This salad, made with tender beef steak, is a variation on the sandwich.

INGREDIENTS

*4 sirloin or round steaks,
about 6 ounces each
1 head of escarole
1 bunch of watercress
4 tomatoes, quartered
4 large cornichons, sliced
4 spring onions, sliced
4 canned artichoke hearts, halved
6 ounces button mushrooms, sliced
12 green olives
½ cup French dressing
salt and freshly ground black
pepper*

SERVES 4

1 Season the steaks with plenty of black pepper and cook on a hot grill, or under a hot broiler , for 4–6 minutes, turning once, until medium rare. Cover and let the steaks rest in a warm place.

2 Combine the salad leaves with all the ingredients except the steak, and toss with the French dressing.

3 Divide the salad among four plates. Slice each steak diagonally and arrange the slices over the salad. Season with salt and fresh black pepper and serve.

SPICED BEEF SATAY

• • •

Tender strips of steak threaded on skewers and spiced with the characteristic flavors of Indonesia are popular with everyone. Tamarind pulp can be found in Asian markets.

INGREDIENTS

1 pound sirloin steak, cut into
½-inch strips
1 teaspoon coriander seeds, dry-
fried and ground
½ teaspoon cumin seeds, dry-fried
and ground
1 teaspoon tamarind pulp
1 small onion
2 garlic cloves
1 tablespoon brown sugar
1 tablespoon dark soy sauce
salt

To serve
cucumber chunks
lemon or lime wedges
Sambal Kecap

MAKES 18 SKEWERS

1 Mix the meat and spices in a large nonmetallic bowl. Soak the tamarind pulp in ⅓ cup water.

2 Strain the tamarind and reserve the juice. Put the onion, garlic, tamarind juice, sugar and soy sauce in a food processor and blend well.

3 Pour the marinade over the meat and spices and toss together well. Let stand for at least 1 hour.

4 Meanwhile, soak some bamboo skewers in water to prevent them from burning while cooking. Thread 5 or 6 pieces of meat onto each skewer and sprinkle with salt. Cook on a hot grill, turning frequently and basting with the marinade, until tender.

5 Serve with cucumber chunks and wedges of lemon or lime for squeezing over the meat. Sambal Kecap is a traditional accompaniment.

SAMBAL KECAP
Mix 1 fresh red chili,
seeded and finely chopped,
2 crushed garlic cloves and
4 tablespoons dark soy sauce with
4 teaspoons lemon juice and
2 tablespoons hot water in a
bowl. Let stand for 30 minutes
before serving.

VEGETABLE-STUFFED BEEF ROLLS

• • •

These Japanese-style beef rolls are very popular for al fresco meals. You could roll up many other vegetables in the sliced beef. Pork is also very good cooked this way.

INGREDIENTS

2 ounces carrot
2 ounces green pepper, seeded
1 bunch of scallions
14 ounces beef round, thinly sliced
all-purpose flour, for dusting
1 tablespoon olive oil
fresh parsley sprigs, to garnish

FOR THE SAUCE
2 tablespoons sugar
3 tablespoons soy sauce
3 tablespoons mirin

SERVES 4

1 Use a sharp knife to shred the carrot and green pepper into 1½- to 2-inch lengths. Wash and peel the outer skins from the scallions, then halve them lengthwise. Shred the scallions diagonally into 1½- to 2-inch lengths.

2 The beef slices should be cut paper thin and measure about 6 inches square. Lay a slice of beef on a chopping board and top with strips of the carrot, green pepper and scallion. Roll up tightly and dust lightly with flour. Repeat with the remaining beef and vegetables.

3 Secure the beef rolls with toothpicks, soaked in water to prevent them from burning, and cook on a medium grill, or in a pan over medium heat, for 10–15 minutes, turning frequently, until golden brown and thoroughly cooked.

4 Blend the ingredients for the sauce in a small pan and heat to dissolve the sugar and form a glaze. Halve the cooked rolls, cutting at a slant, and stand them on a plate with the sloping cut ends facing upward. Dress with the sauce and garnish with fresh parsley.

LAMB STEAKS MARINATED IN MINT AND SHERRY

∘ ∘ ∘

The marinade in this recipe is extremely quick to prepare, and is the key
to its success: the sherry imparts a wonderful tang to the meat.

INGREDIENTS

6 large lamb steaks or
12 smaller chops

FOR THE MARINADE
2 tablespoons chopped fresh mint
leaves
1 tablespoons black peppercorns
1 medium onion, chopped
½ cup sherry
4 tablespoons extra virgin olive oil
2 garlic cloves

SERVES 6

1 Finely chop the mint leaves and peppercorns in a food processor. Add the onion and process again until smooth. Add the rest of the marinade ingredients and process until completely mixed. The marinade should have a thick consistency.

2 Add the marinade to the meat and cover with plastic wrap. Place in the refrigerator to marinate overnight.

3 Cook the steaks on a medium grill for 10–15 minutes, basting occasionally with the marinade.

SKEWERED LAMB WITH CILANTRO YOGURT

· · ·

These Turkish kebabs are traditionally made with lamb, but lean beef or pork works equally well.
You can alternate pieces of bell pepper, lemon or onions with the meat for extra flavor and color.

INGREDIENTS
2 pounds boneless lean lamb
1 large onion, grated
3 bay leaves
5 sprigs of thyme or rosemary
grated rind and juice of 1 lemon
1/2 teaspoon sugar
1/3 cup olive oil
salt and freshly ground black
pepper
sprigs of fresh rosemary, to garnish
barbecued lemon wedges, to serve

FOR THE CILANTRO YOGURT
2/3 cup thick plain yogurt
1 tablespoon chopped fresh mint
1 tablespoon chopped fresh
cilantro
2 teaspoons grated onion

SERVES 4

1 To make the cilantro yogurt, mix together the yogurt, chopped fresh mint, chopped fresh cilantro and grated onion. Transfer the yogurt to a serving bowl.

2 To make the kebabs, cut the lamb into 1-inch cubes and place in a bowl. Mix together the onion, herbs, lemon rind and juice, sugar and oil, then season to taste.

3 Pour the marinade over the meat in the bowl and stir so that the meat is thoroughly covered. Cover with plastic wrap and marinate in the refrigerator for several hours or overnight.

4 Drain the meat and thread onto metal skewers. Cook on a hot grill for about 10 minutes. Garnish with rosemary and grilled lemon wedges and serve with the cilantro yogurt.

LAMB BURGERS WITH RED CURRANT CHUTNEY

• • •

These very special burgers take a little extra time to prepare but are well worth it.
The red currant chutney is the perfect complement to the minty lamb taste.

INGREDIENTS

1¼ pounds ground lean lamb
1 small onion, finely chopped
2 tablespoons finely chopped
fresh mint
2 tablespoons finely chopped
fresh parsley
4 ounces mozzarella cheese
2 tablespoons oil, for basting
salt and freshly ground black
pepper

FOR THE RED CURRANT CHUTNEY
1½ cups fresh or frozen red
currants
2 teaspoons clear honey
1 teaspoon balsamic vinegar
2 tablespoons finely chopped mint

SERVES 4

1 In a large bowl, mix together the ground lamb, chopped onion, mint and parsley until evenly combined. Season well with plenty of salt and freshly ground black pepper.

Cook's Tip

If time is short, or if fresh red currants are not available, serve the burgers with ready-made red currant sauce.

2 Roughly divide the meat mixture into eight equal pieces and use your hands to press each of the pieces into a flat round.

3 Cut the mozzarella into 4 chunks. Place 1 chunk of cheese on half the lamb rounds. Top each one with another round of meat mixture.

4 Press each of the 2 rounds of meat together firmly, making 4 flattish burger shapes. Use your fingers to blend the edges and seal in the cheese completely.

5 Place all the ingredients for the chutney in a bowl and mash them together with a fork. Season well with salt and freshly ground black pepper.

6 Brush the lamb burgers with olive oil and cook them on a moderately hot grill for about 15 minutes, turning once, until golden brown. Serve on hamburger buns with the chutney.

GRILLED LAMB WITH POTATO SLICES

• • •

A traditional mixture of fresh herbs adds a summery flavor to this simple lamb dish.
The leg of lamb will cook more evenly on the grill if it's boned, or "butterflied," first.

INGREDIENTS

1 leg of lamb, about 4½ pounds
1 garlic clove, thinly sliced
handful of fresh flat-leaf parsley
handful of fresh sage
handful of fresh rosemary
handful of fresh thyme
6 tablespoons dry sherry
4 tablespoons walnut oil
1¼ pounds medium-size potatoes
salt and freshly ground
black pepper

SERVES 4

2 Use a sharp kitchen knife to scrape away the meat from the bone on both sides, until the bone is completely exposed. Carefully remove the bone and cut away any sinews and excess fat from the meat.

4 Place the meat in a bowl and pour the sherry and walnut oil over it. Chop half the remaining herbs and sprinkle over the meat. Cover the bowl with a clean dish towel and let marinate in the refrigerator for 30 minutes.

1 Place the lamb on a board, smooth side down, so that you can see where the bone lies. Using a sharp, heavy knife, make a long cut through the flesh down to the bone.

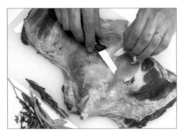

3 Cut through the thickest part of the meat so that you can open it out as flat as possible. (Your butcher can butterfly the meat for you if you prefer.) Then make several cuts in the lamb with a sharp kitchen knife, and push slivers of garlic and sprigs of fresh herbs into the cuts.

5 Remove the lamb from the marinade and season it. Cook on a medium-hot grill for 30–35 minutes, turning occasionally and basting with the reserved marinade.

Cook's Tip

If you have a spit-roasting attachment, the lamb can be rolled and tied with herbs inside, and spit roasted for 1–1½ hours. A spit makes it much easier to cook larger pieces of lamb.

6 Scrub the potatoes, then slice them thickly. Brush with the marinade and place around the lamb. Cook for about 15 minutes, until golden brown.

LAMB WITH LAVENDER BALSAMIC MARINADE

· o ·

Lavender is an unusual flavor to use with meat, but its heady, summery scent works well with grilled lamb. If you prefer, rosemary can take its place.

2 Sprinkle the chopped fresh lavender over the lamb in the bowl.

3 Beat together the vinegar, olive oil and lemon juice and pour over the lamb. Season well with salt and pepper, then turn to coat evenly.

INGREDIENTS

4 racks of lamb, with 3–4 cutlets each
1 shallot, finely chopped
3 tablespoons chopped fresh lavender
1 tablespoon balsamic vinegar
2 tablespoons olive oil
1 tablespoon lemon juice
salt and freshly ground black pepper
handful of lavender sprigs

SERVES 4

1 Place the racks of lamb in a large mixing bowl or wide dish and sprinkle the chopped shallot over them.

4 Sprinkle a few lavender sprigs over the broiler or on the coals of a medium-hot grill. Cook the lamb for 15–20 minutes, turning once and basting with any remaining marinade, until golden brown on the outside and still slightly pink in the center.

LAMB WITH MINT AND LEMON

• • •

*Use this simple and traditional marinade to make the most of fine-quality lamb leg steaks.
Lemon and fresh mint combine extremely well with the flavor of grilled lamb.*

INGREDIENTS

*4 lamb steaks, about 8 ounces each
fresh mint leaves, to garnish*

FOR THE MARINADE
*grated rind and juice of 1/2 lemon
1 garlic clove, crushed
1 scallion, finely chopped
1 teaspoon finely chopped fresh
mint
2 tablespoons extra virgin olive oil
salt and freshly ground black
pepper*

SERVES 4

1 Mix all the marinade ingredients and season to taste. Place the lamb steaks in a shallow dish and add the marinade. Cover with plastic wrap and allow to marinate in the refrigerator for several hours or overnight.

2 Drain the lamb from the marinade and cook on a medium-hot grill for 10–15 minutes or until just cooked, basting occasionally with the marinade and turning once. Garnish the lamb steaks with the fresh mint leaves.

STUFFED EGGPLANT WITH LAMB

• • •

*Ground lamb and eggplant go together beautifully. This is an attractive dish,
with the different-colored peppers in the lightly spiced stuffing mixture.*

INGREDIENTS

2 medium eggplants
2 tablespoons vegetable oil
1 medium onion, sliced
1 teaspoon grated fresh ginger
1 teaspoon chili powder
1 garlic clove, crushed
1/4 teaspoon turmeric
1 teaspoon salt
1 teaspoon ground coriander
1 medium tomato, chopped
12 ounces lean ground lamb
1 medium green bell pepper,
roughly chopped
1 medium orange bell pepper,
roughly chopped
2 tablespoons chopped fresh
cilantro
rice, to serve

FOR THE GARNISH
1/2 onion, sliced
2 cherry tomatoes, quartered
fresh cilantro sprigs

SERVES 4

1 Cut the eggplants in half
lengthwise with a heavy knife. Scoop
out most of the flesh and reserve it for
another dish. Brush the shells with a
little vegetable oil.

2 In a medium saucepan, heat 1
tablespoon oil and fry the sliced onion
until golden brown. Stir in the grated
ginger, chili powder, garlic, turmeric,
salt and coriander. Add the chopped
tomato, lower the heat and cook for
about 5 minutes, stirring constantly.

3 Add the ground lamb to the
saucepan and continue to cook over
medium heat for 7–10 minutes. Stir
in the chopped fresh peppers and the
fresh cilantro.

4 Spoon the lamb mixture into the
eggplant shells and brush the edges
of the shells with the remaining oil.
Cook on a medium grill for 15–20
minutes, until cooked through. Garnish
with sliced onion, cherry tomatoes and
cilantro, and serve with rice, if desired.

VEAL CHOPS WITH BASIL BUTTER

. . .

Veal chops from the loin are an expensive cut and are best cooked quickly and simply.
The flavor of basil goes well with veal, but other herbs can be used instead if you prefer.

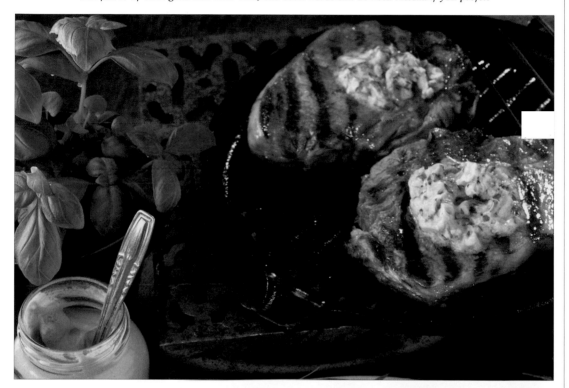

INGREDIENTS

2 tablespoons butter, softened
1 tablespoon Dijon mustard
1 tablespoon chopped fresh basil
olive oil, for brushing
2 veal loin chops, 1-inch thick,
8 ounces each
salt and freshly ground black
pepper
fresh basil sprigs, to garnish

SERVES 2

1 To make the basil butter, cream the softened butter with the Dijon mustard and chopped fresh basil in a large mixing bowl, then season with plenty of freshly ground black pepper.

2 Brush both sides of each chop with olive oil and season with a little salt.

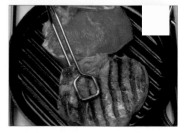

3 Cook the chops on a hot grill for 7–10 minutes, basting with oil and turning once, until done to your liking. (Medium-rare meat will still be slightly soft when pressed, medium meat will be springy, and well-done firm.) Top each chop with half the basil butter and serve at once, garnished with basil.

PORK AND PINEAPPLE SATAY

. . .

This variation on the classic Thai satay has added pineapple, but keeps the traditional coconut and peanut sauce.

INGREDIENTS

1¼ pound pork fillet
1 small onion, chopped
1 garlic clove, chopped
4 tablespoons soy sauce
finely grated rind of ½ lemon
1 teaspoon ground cumin
1 teaspoon ground coriander
1 teaspoon ground turmeric
1 teaspoon dark brown sugar
1 8-ounce can pineapple chunks in juice, or 1 small fresh pineapple, peeled and diced
salt and freshly ground black pepper

FOR THE SATAY SAUCE
¾ cup coconut milk
6 tablespoons crunchy peanut butter
1 garlic clove, crushed
2 teaspoons soy sauce
1 teaspoon dark brown sugar

SERVES 4

2 Place the onion, garlic, soy sauce, lemon rind, spices and sugar in a blender or food processor. Add two pieces of pineapple and process until the mixture is almost smooth.

3 Add to the pork, tossing well to coat evenly. Thread pork onto bamboo skewers (soak skewers in water first), with the remaining pineapple pieces.

4 To make the sauce, pour the coconut milk into a small saucepan and stir in the peanut butter. Stir in the remaining sauce ingredients and heat gently on the grill, stirring, until smooth and hot. Cover and keep warm on the edge of the grill.

5 Cook the pork and pineapple skewers on a medium-hot grill for 10–12 minutes, turning occasionally, until golden brown and thoroughly cooked. Serve with the satay sauce.

1 Using a sharp kitchen knife, trim any fat from the pork fillet and cut it into 1-inch cubes. Place the meat in a large mixing bowl and set aside.

Cook's Tip

You can use creamed coconut, a solid available in blocks at Asian markets, to make the coconut milk. Dissolve a 2-ounce piece in ⅔ cup boiling water and use as above.

LEMONGRASS PORK CHOPS WITH MUSHROOMS

* * *

Thai flavorings are used to make an aromatic marinade and a spicy sauce. The sauce can be put together in a pan on the grill while the chops and mushrooms are cooking.

INGREDIENTS

4 pork chops, about 8 ounces each
4 large field mushrooms
3 tablespoons vegetable oil
4 fresh red chilies, seeded and
finely sliced
3 tablespoons Thai fish sauce
6 tablespoons lime juice
4 shallots, chopped
1 teaspoon roasted ground rice
2 tablespoons chopped scallions
fresh cilantro leaves,
to garnish
4 scallions, shredded,
to garnish

FOR THE MARINADE
2 garlic cloves, chopped
1 tablespoon sugar
1 tablespoon Thai fish sauce
2 tablespoons soy sauce
1 tablespoon sesame oil
1 tablespoon whiskey or dry sherry
2 stalks lemongrass, finely
chopped
2 scallions, chopped

SERVES 4

2 Place the mushrooms and marinated pork chops on a rack and brush with 1 tablespoon vegetable oil. On a medium-hot grill, cook the pork chops for 10–15 minutes and the mushrooms for about 2 minutes, turning once. Brush both with the marinade while cooking.

3 Meanwhile, heat the remaining oil in a small frying pan, then remove from the heat and mix in the remaining ingredients. Put the pork chops and mushrooms on a serving plate and spoon the sauce over them. Garnish with the fresh cilantro leaves and shredded scallions.

1 To make the marinade, mix all the ingredients. Arrange the pork chops in a shallow dish. Pour the marinade over them and let sit for 1–2 hours.

FARMHOUSE PIZZA

• • •

Pizza is not a dish usually associated with barbecue cooking, but in fact the open fire gives the crust a wonderfully crisp texture. Shape the dough to fit the rack of your grill.

INGREDIENTS

6 tablespoons olive oil
8 ounces button mushrooms, sliced
11-ounce package pizza-crust mix
1¼ cups tomato sauce
11 ounces mozzarella cheese, thinly sliced
4 ounces wafer-thin slices smoked ham
6 bottled artichoke hearts in oil, drained and sliced
2-ounce can anchovy fillets, drained and halved lengthwise
10 pitted black olives, halved
2 tablespoons chopped fresh oregano
3 tablespoons freshly grated Parmesan cheese
freshly ground black pepper

SERVES 8

1 Heat 2 tablespoons oil in a pan, add the mushrooms and fry until all the juices have evaporated. Let cool.

2 Make up the pizza dough according to the directions on the package. Roll it out on a floured surface to a 12 × 10-inch rectangle. Brush with oil and place, oiled side down, on a medium-hot grill. Cook for 6 minutes, until firm.

3 Brush the uncooked side of the dough with oil and turn over. Spread with the tomato sauce and arrange the sliced mozzarella on top. Scrunch up the smoked ham and arrange on top of the pizza with the artichoke hearts, anchovies and cooked mushrooms.

4 Dot with the halved olives, then sprinkle with the fresh oregano and Parmesan. Drizzle with the remaining olive oil and season with black pepper. Return to the grill and cook for another 8–10 minutes, or until the dough is golden brown and crisp.

POULTRY
AND GAME

———◆———

Chicken cooked on the grill is unfailingly popular with both adults

and children, and it can be as simple or sophisticated as you choose:

it is very versatile and takes on a whole range of flavors with great

success. Buy breast fillets to make delicious kebabs and salads with a

minimum of preparation, or cook drumsticks and thighs with robust

spicy coatings. Whole birds can be roasted very effectively on a spit,

or they can be flattened out by removing the backbone and cooked on

the grill rack. It is vital to make sure chicken is always very thoroughly

cooked – it needs a medium heat to cook it through without charring

the outside. Don't forget other types of poultry, particularly duck,

which stays beautifully juicy and moist when cooked on the grill.

CHICKEN WITH PINEAPPLE

• • •

The pineapple juice in this Indian recipe is used to tenderize the meat, but it also gives the chicken a deliciously tangy sweetness.

INGREDIENTS

18-ounce can pineapple chunks
in juice
1 teaspoon ground cumin
1 teaspoon ground coriander
1 garlic clove, crushed
1 teaspoon chili powder
1 teaspoon salt
2 tablespoons low-fat plain yogurt
1 tablespoon chopped fresh cilantro
few drops orange food coloring
(optional)
10 ounces skinned, boned chicken
breast and thigh meat, about 2 cups
1/2 red bell pepper
1/2 yellow or green bell pepper
1 large onion
6 cherry tomatoes
1 tablespoon vegetable oil
salad or rice, to serve

SERVES 6

2 In a large bowl, blend together the cumin, ground coriander, garlic, chili powder, salt, yogurt, fresh cilantro and food coloring, if using. Pour in the pineapple juice and mix together.

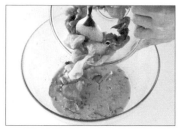

3 Cut the chicken into cubes, add to the yogurt and spice mixture and set aside to marinate for 1–1½ hours. Cut the peppers and onion into chunks.

4 Arrange the chicken pieces, vegetables and reserved pineapple chunks alternately on 6 skewers.

5 Brush the kebabs with oil and cook on a medium grill for about 10 minutes, turning regularly and basting the chicken pieces regularly with the marinade, until cooked through.
Serve with salad or plain cooked rice.

1 Drain the canned pineapple into a bowl. Reserve 12 large chunks of pineapple. Squeeze the juice from the remaining chunks into the bowl, then discard the chunks. You should be left with about ½ cup pineapple juice.

CITRUS KEBABS

• • •

Serve these succulent grilled chicken kebabs on a bed of lettuce leaves, garnished with sprigs of
fresh mint and orange and lemon slices.

INGREDIENTS

4 chicken breasts, skinned and
boned
fresh mint sprigs, to garnish
orange, lemon or lime slices, to
garnish

FOR THE MARINADE
finely grated rind and juice of
½ orange
finely grated rind and juice of
½ lemon or lime
2 tablespoons olive oil
2 tablespoons clear honey
2 tablespoons chopped fresh mint
¼ teaspoon ground cumin
salt and freshly ground black
pepper

SERVES 4

1 Use a heavy knife to cut the chicken into 1-inch cubes.

2 Mix the marinade ingredients together in a large mixing bowl, add the chicken and cover with plastic wrap. Allow to marinate for at least 2 hours, or overnight in the refrigerator.

3 Thread the chicken onto metal skewers and cook on a medium grill for 10 minutes, basting with the marinade and turning frequently. Garnish with mint and citrus slices.

SWEET AND SOUR KEBABS

This marinade contains sugar and will burn very easily, so cook the kebabs slowly and turn them often. Serve these kebabs with Harlequin Rice.

INGREDIENTS

2 chicken breasts, skinned and boned
8 pearl onions or 2 medium onions
4 slices lean bacon
3 firm bananas
1 red bell pepper, diced

FOR THE MARINADE
2 tablespoons brown sugar
1 tablespoon Worcestershire sauce
2 tablespoons lemon juice
salt and freshly ground black pepper

FOR THE HARLEQUIN RICE
2 tablespoons olive oil
1 small red bell pepper, diced
generous 1 cup cooked rice
1 cup cooked peas

SERVES 4

1 Mix together the marinade ingredients. Cut each chicken breast into four pieces, add to the marinade, cover and leave for at least 4 hours, or preferably overnight in the refrigerator.

3 Cut each slice of bacon in half with a sharp knife. Peel the bananas and cut each one into three pieces. Wrap half a bacon rasher around each of the banana pieces.

5 Cook on a low grill for about 15 minutes, turning and basting frequently with the marinade.

6 Meanwhile, heat the oil in a frying pan and stir-fry the diced pepper briefly. Add the rice and peas and stir until heated through. Serve Harlequin Rice with the kebabs.

2 Peel the pearl onions, blanch them in boiling water for 5 minutes and drain. If using medium onions, quarter them after blanching.

4 Thread the bacon and bananas onto metal skewers with the chicken pieces, onions and pepper pieces. Brush generously with the marinade.

BLACKENED CAJUN CHICKEN AND CORN

· · ·

This is a classic Deep South method of cooking in a spiced coating, which can be used for poultry, meat or fish. The coating should begin to char and blacken slightly at the edges.

INGREDIENTS

8 chicken joints (drumsticks, thighs or wings)
2 ears of fresh corn
2 teaspoons garlic salt
2 teaspoons ground black pepper
1½ teaspoons ground cumin
1½ teaspoons paprika
1 teaspoon cayenne pepper
3 tablespoons melted butter
chopped parsley, to garnish

SERVES 4

1 Trim any excess fat from the chicken, but leave the skin in place. Slash the thickest parts with a knife, to allow the flavors to penetrate the meat as much as possible.

2 Pull the husks and silks off the ears of corn, then rinse them under cold running water and pat them dry with paper towels. Cut into thick slices, using a heavy kitchen knife.

3 Mix together all the spices. Brush the chicken and corn with the melted butter and sprinkle the spices over them. Toss well to coat evenly.

4 Cook the chicken pieces on a medium-hot grill for about 25 minutes, turning occasionally. Add the corn after 15 minutes and grill, turning often, until golden brown. Serve garnished with chopped parsley.

CHICKEN WITH HERB AND RICOTTA STUFFING

• • •

These little chicken drumsticks are full of flavor, and the stuffing and bacon help to keep them moist and tender.

INGREDIENTS

4 tablespoons ricotta cheese
1 garlic clove, crushed
3 tablespoons mixed chopped fresh herbs, such as chives, flat-leaf parsley and mint
2 tablespoons fresh brown bread crumbs
8 chicken drumsticks
8 slices lean smoked bacon
1 teaspoon whole-grain mustard
1 tablespoon sunflower oil
salt and freshly ground black pepper

SERVES 4

1 Mix together the ricotta, garlic, herbs and bread crumbs. Season well with plenty of salt and pepper.

2 Carefully loosen the skin from each drumstick and spoon a little of the herb stuffing underneath, smoothing the skin back over firmly.

3 Wrap a bacon slice tightly around the wide end of each drumstick, to hold the skin in place over the stuffing during cooking.

4 Mix together the mustard and oil and brush them over the chicken. Cook on a medium-hot grill for about 25 minutes, turning occasionally.

BABY CHICKENS WITH LIME AND CHILI

• • •

Poussins are small birds that are ideal for one to two portions. The best way to prepare them is spatchcocked—split and flattened out—to ensure more even cooking.

INGREDIENTS

4 poussins or Cornish game hens,
about 1 pound each
3 tablespoons butter
2 tablespoons sun-dried tomato
paste
finely grated rind of 1 lime
2 teaspoons chili sauce
juice of ½ lime
lime wedges, to serve
fresh flat leaf parsley sprigs,
to garnish

SERVES 4

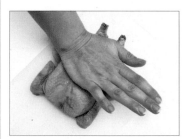

1 Place each poussin or hen on a chopping board, breast side upward, and press down firmly with your hand, to break the breastbone.

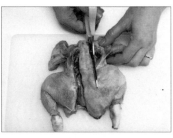

2 Turn the poussin over and, with poultry shears or strong kitchen scissors, cut down either side of the backbone. Remove it and discard.

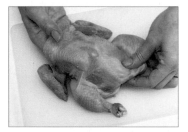

3 Turn the poussin breast side up and flatten it gently. Lift the breast skin carefully and gently ease your fingertips underneath, to loosen it from the flesh.

4 Mix together the butter, sun-dried tomato paste, lime rind and chili sauce in a small bowl. Spread about three-quarters of the mixture under the skin of the poussins, smoothing it evenly over the surface of the flesh.

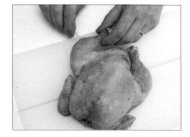

5 To hold the poussins flat during cooking, thread two skewers through each bird, crossing at the center. Each skewer should pass through a drumstick and then out through a wing on the other side.

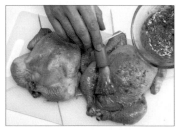

6 Mix the reserved paste with the lime juice and brush it over the skin of the poussins. Cook on a medium-hot grill, turning occasionally, for 25–30 minutes, or until there is no trace of pink in the juices when the flesh is pierced. Garnish with lime wedges and fresh flat leaf parsley.

CHICKEN COOKED IN SPICES AND COCONUT

This chicken dish can be prepared in advance until you are ready to light the grill. Serve it with naan (a flat, leavened Indian bread). Creamed coconut can be found in Asian markets.

INGREDIENTS

7-ounce block creamed
 coconut
1¼ cups boiling water
3 garlic cloves, chopped
2 scallions, chopped
1 fresh green chili, chopped
2-inch piece fresh ginger,
 chopped
1 teaspoon fennel seeds
½ teaspoon black peppercorns
seeds from 4 cardamom pods
2 tablespoons ground coriander
1 teaspoon ground cumin
1 teaspoon ground star anise
1 teaspoon ground nutmeg
½ teaspoon ground cloves
½ teaspoon ground turmeric
4 large chicken breasts, skinned
 and boned
onion rings and fresh cilantro
 sprigs, to garnish

SERVES 4

2 Make several diagonal cuts across the chicken breasts. Arrange in a layer in a shallow dish. Spoon on half the coconut mixture and toss well to coat evenly. Cover the dish and let the chicken marinate for at least 30 minutes, or overnight in the refrigerator.

3 Cook the chicken on a medium grill for 12–15 minutes, turning once, until well browned and thoroughly cooked. Heat the remaining coconut mixture gently until boiling. Serve with the chicken, garnished with onion rings and sprigs of cilantro.

1 Break up the coconut and put it in a bowl. Pour the boiling water over it and set aside to dissolve. Place the chopped garlic, scallions, chili, ginger and all of the spices in a blender or food processor. Pour in the coconut mixture and blend to a smooth paste.

GRILLED CASHEW CHICKEN

• • •

*This dish comes from the beautiful Indonesian island of Bali, where nuts are widely used as a
base for sauces and marinades. Serve it with a green salad and a hot chili dipping sauce.*

INGREDIENTS

4 chicken legs
radishes, sliced, to garnish
1/2 cucumber, sliced, to garnish
Chinese cabbage, to serve

FOR THE MARINADE
*2 ounces raw cashew or
macadamia nuts*
*2 shallots, or 1 small onion, finely
chopped*
2 garlic cloves, crushed
2 small red chilies, chopped
2-inch piece lemongrass
1 tablespoon tamarind sauce
2 tablespoons dark soy sauce
1 tablespoon Thai fish sauce
2 teaspoons sugar
1/2 teaspoon salt
*1 tablespoon rice or white wine
vinegar*

SERVES 4

1 Using a sharp kitchen knife, slash
the chicken legs several times through
to the bone. Chop off the knuckle end
and discard.

2 To make the marinade, place the
cashew or macadamia nuts in a food
processor and grind until fine (or use
a pestle and mortar to grind them).

3 Add the chopped shallots or onion,
garlic, chilies and lemongrass and
blend. Add the remaining marinade
ingredients and blend again.

4 Spread the marinade over the
chicken and leave for up to 8 hours
in the refrigerator. Cook the chicken on
a medium grill for 25 minutes, basting
and turning occasionally. Garnish with
radishes and cucumber and serve on a
bed of Chinese cabbage.

HOT AND SOUR CHICKEN SALAD

• • •

This chicken salad from Vietnam is equally delicious made with shrimp.
Allow one pound of fresh shrimp tails to serve four people.

INGREDIENTS

2 chicken breasts, skinned and
boned
4 ounces bean sprouts
1 head Chinese cabbage, shredded
2 medium carrots, cut into
matchsticks
1 red onion, thinly sliced
2 large gherkins, sliced

FOR THE MARINADE
1 small red chili, seeded and finely
chopped
1/2-in piece fresh ginger, chopped
1 garlic clove, crushed
1 tablespoon crunchy peanut
butter
2 tablespoons chopped fresh
cilantro
1 teaspoon sugar
1/2 teaspoon salt
1 tablespoon rice or white wine
vinegar
4 tablespoons vegetable oil
2 teaspoons Thai fish sauce

SERVES 4–6

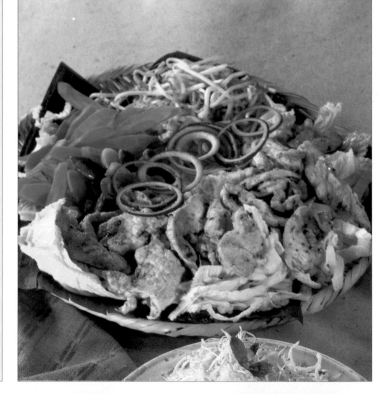

1 Slice the chicken breasts thinly
and place in a shallow bowl. Grind
the chili, ginger and garlic in a food
processor (or grind using a mortar and
pestle), then add the peanut butter,
chopped fresh cilantro, sugar and salt.

2 Add the rice or white wine vinegar,
2 tablespoons of the oil and the fish
sauce to the ingredients in the food
processor. Combine well. Cover the
chicken with the spice mixture and
let it marinate for at least 2–3 hours.

3 Cook the chicken on a medium-
hot grill or in a frying pan on the stove
for about 5 minutes, basting often and
turning once. Arrange the salad
ingredients on a serving dish and top
with the cooked chicken.

CHICKEN SALAD WITH LAVENDER AND HERBS

. . .

The delightful scent of lavender has a natural affinity with garlic, orange, and fresh herbs. The addition of fried polenta makes this salad filling as well as delicious.

INGREDIENTS

4 boneless chicken breasts
3¾ cups light chicken stock
1 cup fine polenta or cornmeal
4 tablespoons butter, plus extra for greasing
1 pound young spinach
6 ounces lamb's lettuce
8 sprigs fresh lavender
8 small tomatoes, halved
salt and freshly ground black pepper

FOR THE MARINADE
6 fresh lavender flowers
2 teaspoons finely grated orange zest
2 garlic cloves, crushed
2 teaspoons clear honey
2 tablespoons olive oil
2 teaspoons chopped fresh thyme
2 teaspoons chopped fresh marjoram
salt

SERVES 4

1 To make the marinade, strip the lavender flowers from the stems and combine with the orange zest, garlic, honey and salt. Add the oil and herbs. Slash the chicken deeply, spread the mixture over it and let it marinate in the refrigerator for 20 minutes.

2 To make the polenta, bring the chicken stock to a boil in a heavy saucepan. Add the cornmeal in a steady stream, stirring all the time, until thick. Turn the cooked polenta out onto a shallow buttered platter and let it cool.

3 Cook the chicken on a medium grill or under the broiler for about 15 minutes, basting with the marinade and turning once, until cooked through.

4 Cut the polenta into 1-inch cubes using a wet knife. Heat the butter in a large frying pan and fry the polenta until golden.

5 Divide the salad leaves between four dinner plates. Slice each chicken breast and arrange over the salad. Arrange the polenta among the salad, decorate with sprigs of lavender and tomato halves, season with salt and freshly ground black pepper and serve.

CHICKEN SALAD WITH CILANTRO DRESSING

• • •

Serve this salad warm to make the most of the wonderful flavor of grilled chicken basted with a marinade of coriander, sesame and mustard.

INGREDIENTS

4 medium chicken breasts, skinned
and boned
8 ounces snow peas
2 heads decorative lettuce such
as lollo rosso or oak leaf
3 carrots, cut into matchsticks
6 ounces button mushrooms, sliced
6 slices bacon, fried and chopped

FOR THE CILANTRO DRESSING
1/2 cup lemon juice
2 tablespoons whole-grain mustard
1 cup olive oil
1/3 cup sesame oil
1 teaspoon coriander seeds,
crushed
1 tablespoon chopped fresh
cilantro, to garnish

SERVES 6

1 Mix all the dressing ingredients in a bowl. Place the chicken breasts in a dish and pour half the dressing over them. Marinate overnight in the refrigerator; refrigerate the remaining dressing.

2 Cook the snow peas in boiling water for 2 minutes, then refresh in cold water. Tear the lettuces into small pieces and mix all the other salad ingredients and the bacon together. Arrange the salad in individual bowls.

3 Cook the chicken breasts on a medium grill for 10–15 minutes, basting with the marinade and turning once, until cooked through. Slice them on the diagonal into thin pieces. Divide among the bowls of salad and add some dressing to each dish. Combine quickly and sprinkle some fresh cilantro over each bowl.

MARYLAND SALAD

. . .

*Grilled chicken, corn, bacon, banana and watercress combine here
in a sensational main course salad. Serve with buttered baked potatoes.*

INGREDIENTS

*4 boneless chicken breasts
olive oil, for brushing
8 ounces rindless unsmoked bacon
4 ears of fresh corn
3 tablespoons melted butter
4 ripe bananas, peeled and halved
4 tomatoes, halved
1 head escarole or Boston lettuce
1 bunch watercress
salt and freshly ground black
pepper*

FOR THE DRESSING
*5 tablespoons peanut oil
1 tablespoon white wine vinegar
2 teaspoons maple syrup
2 teaspoons mild mustard*

SERVES 4

3 Combine the dressing ingredients
with 1 tablespoon water in a screw-
top jar and shake well to mix. Wash
and spin the lettuce leaves, then toss
the salad with the dressing.

4 Divide the dressed salad among
four large plates. Slice the chicken and
arrange it on top of the salad with the
bacon, banana, corn and tomatoes.
Season well and serve.

1 Season the chicken breasts, brush
with oil and cook on a medium grill or
under the broiler for 15–20 minutes,
turning once. Cook the bacon for 8–10
minutes, or until crisp.

2 Bring a large pan of water to a boil
and cook the corn for about 5 minutes,
until tender. For extra flavor, brush
with butter and brown on the grill.
Grill the bananas and tomatoes for 6–8
minutes: Brush these with butter too if
you wish.

THAI GRILLED CHICKEN

* * *

Thai grilled chicken is especially delicious when cooked outdoors on the barbecue.
Serve it on a bed of crisp salad with lime wedges to offset its richness.

INGREDIENTS

2 pounds chicken drumsticks or
thighs
salt and freshly ground
black pepper
crisp lettuce leaves, to serve
1/2 cucumber, cut into strips,
to garnish
4 scallions, trimmed,
to garnish
2 limes, quartered, to garnish

FOR THE MARINADE
1 teaspoon black peppercorns
1/2 teaspoon caraway or cumin
seeds
4 teaspoons sugar
2 teaspoons paprika
3/4-inch piece fresh ginger, chopped
3 garlic cloves, crushed
1 tablespoon finely chopped fresh
cilantro, white root or stem
3 tablespoons vegetable oil

SERVES 4–6

1 Chop through the narrow end of each drumstick with a heavy knife. Score the chicken pieces deeply to allow the marinade to penetrate and arrange in a shallow bowl.

2 Grind the peppercorns, caraway or cumin seeds and sugar with a mortar and pestle or in a food processor. Add the paprika, ginger, garlic, cilantro and oil and grind to a paste.

3 Spread the marinade over the chicken and let marinate in the refrigerator for 6 hours. Cook the chicken on a medium grill for about 20 minutes, basting with the marinade and turning once. Season, arrange on a bed of lettuce and garnish before serving.

MEDITERRANEAN TURKEY SKEWERS

· · ·

*These attractive kebabs can be assembled in advance and left to marinate until you are ready
to cook them. Grilling intensifies the Mediterranean flavors of the vegetables.*

INGREDIENTS

2 medium zucchini
1 long thin eggplant
*11 ounces boneless turkey, cut
into 2-inch cubes*
12–16 pearl onions
*1 red or yellow bell pepper, cut
into 2-inch squares*

FOR THE MARINADE
6 tablespoons olive oil
3 tablespoons fresh lemon juice
1 garlic clove, finely chopped
*2 tablespoons chopped fresh basil
salt and freshly ground black
pepper*

SERVES 4

3 Prepare the skewers by alternating
the turkey, onions and pepper pieces.
Lay the prepared skewers on a platter
and sprinkle with the flavored oil.
Allow to marinate for 30 minutes.

4 Cook on a medium grill or
under a broiler, turning the skewers
occasionally, for about 10 minutes,
or until the turkey is cooked and the
vegetables are tender.

1 To make the marinade, mix the
olive oil with the lemon juice, garlic
and chopped fresh basil. Season well
with plenty of salt and black pepper.

2 Slice the zucchini and eggplant
lengthwise into strips ¼ inch thick. Cut
them crosswise about two-thirds down
their length. Discard the shorter
lengths. Wrap half the turkey pieces
with the zucchini slices and the other
half with the eggplant slices.

QUAIL WITH A FIVE-SPICE MARINADE

° ° °

Blending and grinding your own five-spice powder for this Vietnamese dish will give the freshest-tasting results. If you are short of time, buy a ready-mixed blend from the supermarket.

INGREDIENTS

6 quail, cleaned
2 scallions, roughly chopped,
to garnish
mandarin orange or satsuma,
to garnish
banana leaves, to serve

FOR THE MARINADE
2 pieces star anise
2 teaspoons ground cinnamon
2 teaspoons fennel seeds
2 teaspoons Sichuan pepper
a pinch ground cloves
1 small onion, finely chopped
1 garlic clove, crushed
4 tablespoons clear honey
2 tablespoons dark soy sauce

SERVES 4–6

1 Remove the backbones from the quail by cutting down each side with a pair of strong kitchen scissors.

2 Flatten the birds with the palm of your hand and secure each bird using two bamboo skewers.

3 To make the marinade, place the five spices in a spice mill and grind into a fine powder (or grind using a mortar and pestle). Add the chopped onion, garlic, clear honey and soy sauce, and combine until thoroughly mixed.

4 Arrange the quail on a flat dish and pour the marinade over them. Cover the dish with plastic wrap and let the quail marinate in the refrigerator for 8 hours or overnight.

5 Cook the quail on a medium grill for 15–20 minutes, until golden brown, basting occasionally with the marinade and turning once.

6 To garnish, remove the outer zest from the mandarin orange or satsuma, using a vegetable peeler. Shred the zest finely and combine with the chopped scallions. Arrange the quail on a bed of banana leaves and garnish with the orange zest and scallions.

Cook's Tip

If you prefer, or if quail are not available, you could use other poultry, such as poussins or Cornish game hens, as a substitute.

PHEASANT WITH SAGE AND LEMON

∘ ∘ ∘

Pheasant is quick to cook and makes a very special summer meal.
This recipe can also be used for guinea fowl.

INGREDIENTS

2 pheasant, about 1 pound each
1 lemon
4 tablespoons chopped fresh sage
3 shallots
1 teaspoon Dijon mustard
1 tablespoon brandy or dry sherry
1²/₃ cup crème fraîche
salt and freshly ground black
pepper
lemon wedges and sage sprigs, to
garnish

SERVES 4

2 Finely grate the rind from half the lemon and slice the rest thinly. Mix together the lemon rind and half the chopped sage in a small bowl.

5 Meanwhile, cook the shallots on the grill for 10–12 minutes, turning occasionally, until the skin is blackened and the inside very soft. Peel off the skins, chop the flesh roughly and mash it with the Dijon mustard and brandy or sherry.

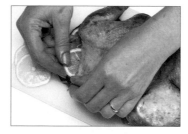

1 Place the pheasant, breast side up, on a chopping board and cut them in half lengthwise, using poultry shears or a sharp kitchen knife.

3 Loosen the skin on the breasts and legs of the pheasant and push a little of the sage mixture underneath. Tuck the lemon slices under the skin, smoothing the skin back firmly.

6 Stir in the crème fraîche and add the reserved chopped sage. Season with plenty of salt and freshly ground black pepper. Serve the dressing with the pheasant, garnished with lemon wedges and sprigs of fresh sage.

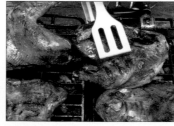

4 Place the half pheasants on a medium-hot grill and cook for 25–30 minutes, turning once.

Cook's Tip

Try to choose pheasant
with undamaged skins, so that
the flavorings stay in place
during cooking.

Spiced Duck with Pears

○ ○ ○

This delicious casserole can be cooked on the grill or the stove. The browned pears are added toward the end of cooking, along with a pine nut and garlic paste to flavor and thicken.

INGREDIENTS

6 duck portions, either breast or leg pieces
1 tablespoon olive oil
1 large onion, thinly sliced
1 cinnamon stick, halved
2 thyme sprigs
2 cups duck or chicken stock
mashed potato and green vegetable (optional), to serve

To FINISH

3 firm ripe pears, peeled and cored
2 tablespoons olive oil
2 garlic cloves, sliced
1/3 cup pine nuts
1/2 teaspoon saffron strands
2 tablespoons raisins
salt and freshly ground black pepper
thyme sprigs or parsley, to garnish

Serves 6

1 Fry the duck portions in olive oil for 5 minutes, until golden, or brush the portions with oil and cook them on a hot grill for 8–10 minutes. Transfer the duck to a large flameproof dish. If frying, drain off all but 1 tablespoon of the fat left in the pan.

2 Fry the onion in the frying pan for 5 minutes, until golden. Add the cinnamon stick, thyme and stock and bring to a boil. Pour over the duck in the dish and cook slowly on a low grill for about 1 hour and 15 minutes.

3 Halve the pears, brush with oil and grill until brown, or fry them in the oil on the stove. Pound the garlic, pine nuts and saffron with a mortar and pestle, to make a thick, smooth paste.

4 Add the paste, raisins and pears to the flameproof dish. Cook for 15 minutes, until the pears are tender.

5 Season to taste and garnish with the fresh herbs. Serve with mashed potatoes and a green vegetable, if desired.

Cook's Tip

A good stock is essential for this dish. Buy a large duck (plus two extra duck breasts if you want portions to be generous) and joint it yourself, using the giblets and carcass for stock. If you buy duck portions, use a flavorful chicken stock.

APRICOT DUCK WITH BEAN SPROUT SALAD

. . .

Duck is rich in fat, so it stays beautifully moist when cooked on a grill,
while any excess fat drains away.

INGREDIENTS

4 plump duck breasts, with skin
1 small red onion, thinly sliced
3/4 cup dried apricots
1 tablespoon clear honey
1 teaspoon sesame oil
2 teaspoons ground star anise
salt and freshly ground black
pepper

FOR THE SALAD
1/2 head Chinese cabbage, finely
shredded
2 cups beans sprouts
2 scallions, shredded
1 tablespoon light soy sauce
1 tablespoon peanut oil
1 teaspoon sesame oil
1 teaspoon clear honey

SERVES 4

2 Tuck the slices of onion and the apricots inside the pocket and press the breast firmly back into shape. Secure with metal skewers.

3 Mix together the honey and sesame oil and brush generously over the duck, particularly the skin. Sprinkle with the star anise and season with plenty of salt and fresh black pepper.

4 To make the salad, mix together the shredded Chinese cabbage, bean sprouts and shredded scallions in a large bowl.

5 Shake together all the salad dressing ingredients in a screw-top jar. Season to taste with salt and pepper. Toss into the salad.

6 Cook the duck over a medium-hot grill for 12–15 minutes, turning once, until golden brown. The duck should be slightly pink in the center.

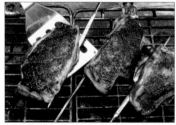

Cook's Tip

If you prefer not to eat the bean sprouts raw, they can be blanched by plunging them into boiling water for 1 minute. Drain and refresh in cold water.

1 Place the duck breasts, skin side down, on a chopping board or clean work surface and cut a long slit down one side with a sharp kitchen knife, cutting not quite through, to form a large pocket.

DUCK BREASTS WITH RED PEPPER JELLY GLAZE

° ° °

Sweet potatoes have pinkish skins and flesh varying from creamy white to deep orange.
Choose a long, cylindrical tuber to make neat round slices for this Cajun dish.

INGREDIENTS

2 duck breasts
1 sweet potato, about 14 ounces
2 tablespoons red pepper jelly
1 tablespoon sherry vinegar
4 tablespoons butter, melted
coarse sea salt and freshly ground
black pepper

SERVES 2

4 Meanwhile, warm the red pepper jelly and sherry vinegar together in a bowl set over a saucepan of hot water, stirring to mix them as the jelly melts. Brush the skin of the duck with this jelly glaze and return to the grill, skin side down, for another 2–3 minutes to caramelize it.

5 Brush the sweet potato slices with melted butter and sprinkle with coarse sea salt. Cook on a hot grill for 8–10 minutes, until soft, brushing with more butter and sprinkling with salt and pepper when you turn them. Serve the duck sliced with the sweet potatoes and accompany with a green salad.

1 Slash the skin of the duck breasts diagonally at 1-inch intervals and rub plenty of salt and pepper over the skin and into the cuts.

2 Scrub the sweet potato and cut into ½-inch slices, discarding the ends.

3 Cook the duck breasts on a medium grill, skin side down, for 5 minutes. Turn and cook for another 8–10 minutes, according to how pink you like your duck.

DUCK BREASTS WITH RED PLUMS

· · ·

The rich fruity sauce for this dish combines brandy and red plums with heavy cream and cilantro. The sauce can be made in a pan on the grill while the duck is cooking.

INGREDIENTS

*4 duck breasts, about 6 ounces
each, skinned*
2 teaspoons crushed cinnamon stick
4 tablespoons butter
*1 tablespoon plum brandy or
cognac*
1 cup chicken stock
1 cup heavy cream
6 fresh red plums, pitted and sliced
*6 sprigs fresh cilantro leaves, plus
extra to garnish*
*salt and freshly ground black
pepper*

SERVES 4

1 Score the duck breasts and sprinkle with salt. Press the crushed cinnamon onto both sides of the duck breasts. Brush with butter and cook on a medium grill for 15–20 minutes, turning once, until the duck is tender.

2 To make the sauce, melt half the remaining butter in a saucepan. Add the brandy or cognac and set it alight. When the flames have died down, add the stock and cream and allow to simmer gently until reduced and thickened. Add seasoning to taste.

3 In a saucepan, melt the other half of the butter and fry the plums with the cilantro just enough to cook the fruit through. Slice the duck breasts and pour some sauce around each one, then garnish with the plum slices and the chopped fresh cilantro.

JUNIPER-SPICED VENISON CHOPS

. . .

Depending on the type of venison available, the chops will vary in size,
so you will need either one or two per person.

INGREDIENTS

4–8 venison chops
1 cup red wine
2 medium red onions
6 juniper berries, crushed
1 cinnamon stick, crumbled
1 dried bay leaf, crumbled
thinly pared strip of orange rind
olive oil, for brushing
salt and freshly ground black
pepper

SERVES 4

2 Add the juniper berries, cinnamon, bay leaf and orange rind. Toss well to coat evenly and then cover the bowl and allow to marinate for at least an hour, or overnight in the refrigerator.

1 Place the venison chops in a large mixing bowl and pour the red wine over them. Using a sharp knife, cut the red onions in half crosswise and add them to the bowl.

3 Drain the venison and onions and reserve the marinade. Brush the venison and onions generously with the olive oil and sprinkle with plenty of salt and freshly ground black pepper.

4 Cook the venison and onions on a medium-hot grill for 8–10 minutes on each side, turning once and basting regularly with the marinade. The venison should still be slightly pink inside even when fully cooked.

Cook's Tip
Tender farmed venison
is now widely available
from supermarkets and good
butcher shops, but if you can't
find it, beef steaks could be
used instead.

Fish and Seafood

Cooking over charcoal adds a marvellous flavor to fish and seafood, and it's very quick and easy to prepare this way. Oily fish such as mackerel, sardines or tuna are perfectly suited to broiling and won't dry out, while charbroiling will enhance their robust flavors. Use plump shrimps or firm meaty-textured fish such as monkfish or swordfish for kebabs, but marinate them first to keep them moist. More delicate fish, or those that are best cooked in their own steam, can also be grilled very successfully: just wrap them securely in aluminum foil and cook them either on the rack or directly on the coals. You can include all kinds of flavorings in the foil parcels, too.

SPICED SHRIMP WITH VEGETABLES

• • •

This is a light and nutritious Indian dish, excellent served either on a bed of lettuce leaves, or with plain boiled rice or chapatis (flat rounds of unleavened bread, available in Asian markets).

INGREDIENTS
20 cooked jumbo shrimp, peeled
1 medium zucchini, thickly sliced
1 medium onion, cut into 8 chunks
8 cherry tomatoes
8 ears of baby corn
mixed salad leaves, to serve

FOR THE MARINADE
2 tablespoons chopped fresh
cilantro
1 teaspoon salt
2 fresh green chilies, seeded
if desired
3 tablespoons lemon juice
2 tablespoons vegetable oil

SERVES 4

1 To make the marinade, blend the cilantro, salt, chilies, lemon juice and oil together in a food processor.

2 Transfer the contents of the food processor to a bowl.

3 Add the peeled shrimp to the mixture in the bowl and stir to make sure that all the shrimp are well coated. Cover the bowl with plastic wrap and set aside in a cool place to marinate for about 30 minutes.

4 Arrange the vegetables and shrimp alternately on 4 long skewers. Cook on a medium grill for 5 minutes, turning frequently, until cooked and browned. Serve immediately, on a bed of mixed salad leaves.

JUMBO SHRIMP SKEWERS WITH WALNUT PESTO

• • •

This is an unusual appetizer or main course, which can be prepared in advance and kept in the refrigerator until you're ready to cook it.

INGREDIENTS

12–16 raw, unshelled jumbo shrimp
1/2 cup walnut pieces
4 tablespoons chopped fresh
flat-leaf parsley
4 tablespoons chopped fresh basil
2 garlic cloves, chopped
3 tablespoons grated fresh
Parmesan cheese
2 tablespoons extra virgin olive oil
2 tablespoons walnut oil
salt and freshly ground black
pepper

SERVES 4

3 Add half the pesto to the shrimp in the bowl, toss them well, then cover and chill in the refrigerator for a minimum of 1 hour, or overnight.

4 Thread the shrimp onto skewers and cook them on a hot grill for 3–4 minutes, turning once. Serve with the remaining pesto and a green salad.

1 Peel the shrimp, removing the heads but leaving the tails. Devein and then put the shrimp in a large mixing bowl.

2 To make the pesto, place the walnuts, parsley, basil, garlic, cheese and oils in a food processor and process until finely chopped. Season.

MACKEREL KEBABS WITH SWEET PEPPER SALAD

• • •

Mackerel is an excellent fish for grilling because its natural oils keep it moist and tasty.
This recipe combines mackerel with peppers and tomatoes in a flavorful summer salad.

INGREDIENTS

4 medium mackerel, about
8 ounces each, filleted
2 small red onions, cut into wedges
2 tablespoons chopped fresh
marjoram
4 tablespoons dry white wine
3 tablespoons olive oil
juice of 1 lime

FOR THE SALAD
1 red bell pepper
1 yellow bell pepper
1 small red onion
2 large plum tomatoes
1 tablespoon chopped fresh
marjoram
2 teaspoons balsamic vinegar
salt and freshly ground black
pepper

SERVES 4

2 Mix together the marjoram, wine, oil and lime juice and spoon over the fish. Cover and chill in the refrigerator for at least 30 minutes, turning once.

3 To make the salad, quarter and seed both peppers and halve the onion. Place the peppers and onion, skin side down, with the whole tomatoes on a hot grill and cook until the skins are blackened and charred.

4 Remove the vegetables from the grill and set aside until they are cool enough to handle. Use a sharp knife to peel off and discard the skins.

5 Chop the vegetables roughly and put them in a bowl. Stir in the marjoram and balsamic vinegar and season to taste. Toss thoroughly.

6 Remove the kebabs from the refrigerator and cook on a hot grill for 10–12 minutes, turning occasionally and basting with the marinade. Serve with the pepper salad.

1 Thread each mackerel fillet onto a skewer, with an onion wedge on each end. Arrange the skewers in a dish.

Cook's Tip
Other oily fish can be used for this dish: try fillets or cubes of herring, rainbow trout or salmon, instead.

SWORDFISH KEBABS

Swordfish has a firm, meaty texture that makes it ideal for cooking on the grill. Marinate the fish first to keep it moist.

INGREDIENTS

2 pounds swordfish steaks
3 tablespoons olive oil
juice of ½ lemon
1 garlic clove, crushed
1 teaspoon paprika
3 tomatoes, quartered
2 onions, cut into wedges
salt and freshly ground black pepper
salad and pita bread, to serve

SERVES 4–6

1 Use a large kitchen knife to cut the swordfish steaks into large cubes. Arrange the cubes in a single layer in a large shallow dish.

2 Blend together the olive oil, lemon juice, garlic, paprika and seasoning in a bowl, and pour the mixture over the fish. Cover the dish loosely with plastic wrap and allow to marinate in a cool place for up to 2 hours.

3 Thread the fish cubes onto metal skewers, alternating them with the pieces of tomato and onion wedges.

4 Cook the kebabs on a hot grill for 5–10 minutes, basting frequently with the remaining marinade and turning occasionally. Serve with salad and pita bread.

CALAMARI WITH TWO-TOMATO STUFFING

· · ·

Calamari, or baby squid, cook very quickly; be sure to turn and baste them often and take care not to overcook them.

INGREDIENTS

1¼ pounds baby squid, cleaned
1 garlic clove, crushed
3 plum tomatoes, skinned and chopped
8 sun-dried tomatoes in oil, drained and chopped
4 tablespoons chopped fresh basil, plus extra, to serve
4 tablespoons fresh white bread crumbs
3 tablespoons olive oil
1 tablespoon red wine vinegar
salt and freshly ground black pepper
lemon juice, to serve

SERVES 4

1 Remove the tentacles from the squid and roughly chop them; leave the main part of the squid whole.

2 Mix together the crushed garlic, plum tomatoes, sun-dried tomatoes, chopped fresh basil and bread crumbs. Stir in 1 tablespoon of the olive oil and the vinegar. Season with plenty of salt and freshly ground black pepper. Soak some wooden toothpicks in water for 10 minutes before use, to prevent them from burning on the grill.

3 Using a teaspoon, fill the squid with the stuffing mixture. Secure the open ends with the toothpicks to hold the stuffing mixture in place.

4 Brush the squid with the remaining olive oil and cook over a medium-hot grill for 4–5 minutes, turning often. Sprinkle with lemon juice and extra chopped fresh basil to serve.

GRILLED SCALLOPS WITH LIME BUTTER

• • •

Fresh scallops cook quickly, so they're ideal for barbecues. This recipe combines them simply with lime and fennel.

INGREDIENTS

1 fennel bulb
2 limes
12 large scallops, cleaned
1 egg yolk
6 tablespoons melted butter
olive oil for brushing
salt and freshly ground
black pepper

SERVES 4

3 Place the egg yolk and remaining lime rind and juice in a small bowl and whisk until pale and smooth.

5 Brush the fennel wedges with olive oil and cook them on a hot grill for 3–4 minutes, turning once.

1 Trim any feathery leaves from the fennel and reserve them. Slice the bulb lengthwise into thin wedges.

4 Gradually whisk in the melted butter and continue whisking until thick and smooth. Finely chop the reserved fennel leaves and stir them in, with seasoning to taste.

6 Add the scallops and cook for another 3–4 minutes, turning once. Serve with the lime and fennel butter and the lime wedges.

2 Cut one lime into wedges. Finely grate the rind and squeeze the juice from the other lime; toss half the juice and rind with the scallops. Season well with salt and fresh black pepper.

Cook's Tip
If the scallops are small, you may wish to thread them onto flat skewers to make turning them easier.

SARDINES WITH WARM HERB SALSA

• • •

Plain grilling is the very best way to cook fresh sardines. Served with this luscious herb salsa, the only other essential item is fresh, crusty bread, to mop up the tasty juices.

INGREDIENTS

12–16 fresh sardines
oil, for brushing
juice of 1 lemon

FOR THE SALSA

1 tablespoon butter
4 scallions, chopped
1 garlic clove, finely chopped
rind of 1 lemon
2 tablespoons finely chopped
fresh parsley
2 tablespoons finely snipped
fresh chives
2 tablespoons finely chopped
fresh basil
2 tablespoon green olive paste
2 teaspoons balsamic vinegar
salt and freshly ground black
pepper

SERVES 4

1 To clean the sardines, use a pair of small kitchen scissors to slit the fish along the belly and pull out the intestines. Wipe the fish with paper towels and then arrange on a grill rack.

2 To make the salsa, melt the butter in a small pan and gently sauté the scallions and garlic for about 2 minutes, shaking the pan occasionally, until softened but not browned.

3 Add the lemon rind and remaining salsa ingredients to the scallions and garlic in the pan and keep warm on the edge of the grill, stirring occasionally. Do not allow to boil.

4 Brush the sardines lightly with oil and sprinkle with lemon juice, salt and pepper. Cook for about 2 minutes on each side, over moderate heat. Serve with the warm salsa and crusty bread.

STUFFED SARDINES

• • •

This Middle Eastern–inspired dish doesn't take much preparation and is a meal in itself.
Just serve with a crisp green salad tossed in a fresh lemon vinaigrette to make it complete.

INGREDIENTS

1 tablespoon fresh parsley
3–4 garlic cloves, crushed
8–12 fresh or frozen sardines,
prepared
2 tablespoons lemon juice
½ cup flour
½ teaspoon ground cumin
olive oil, for brushing
salt and freshly ground black
pepper
nan bread and green salad,
to serve

SERVES 4

1 Finely chop the parsley and mix in a small bowl with the garlic. Pat the parsley and garlic mixture all over the outsides and insides of the sardines. Sprinkle the sardines with the lemon juice and set aside, in a dish covered with a clean dish cloth, in a cool place for about 2 hours to absorb the flavors.

2 Place the flour on a large plate and season with cumin, salt and pepper. Roll the sardines in the seasoned flour.

3 Brush the sardines with olive oil and cook on a medium-hot grill for about 3 minutes on each side. Serve with nan bread and a green salad.

MONKFISH WITH PEPPERED CITRUS MARINADE

∘ ∘ ∘

Monkfish is a firm, meaty fish that keeps its shape well when cooked on the grill.
Serve with a green salad.

INGREDIENTS
2 monkfish tails, about
12 ounces each
1 lime
1 lemon
2 oranges
handful of fresh thyme sprigs
2 tablespoons olive oil
1 tablespoon mixed peppercorns,
roughly crushed
salt and freshly ground
black pepper

SERVES 4

2 Turn the fish and repeat on the other side, to remove the second fillet. Repeat on the second tail. (If you prefer, you can ask your fishmonger to do this for you.) Lay the 4 fillets out flat on a chopping board.

5 Squeeze the juice from the citrus fruits and mix it with the olive oil and more salt and pepper. Spoon over the fish. Cover with plastic wrap and marinate in the refrigerator for about 1 hour, turning occasionally and spooning the marinade over the fish.

1 Using a sharp kitchen knife, remove any skin from the monkfish tails. Cut carefully down one side of the backbone, sliding the knife between the bone and the flesh, to remove the fillet on one side.

3 Cut two slices from each of the citrus fruits and arrange them over 2 of the fillets. Add a few sprigs of fresh thyme and sprinkle with plenty of salt and freshly ground black pepper. Finely grate the rind from the remaining fruit and sprinkle it over the fish.

6 Drain the monkfish, reserving the marinade, and sprinkle with the crushed peppercorns. Cook on a medium-hot grill for 15–20 minutes, basting with the marinade and turning occasionally, until the fish is evenly cooked. Serve immediately.

4 Lay the other 2 fillets on top and tie them firmly at intervals.

SMOKED MACKEREL WITH BLUEBERRIES

• • •

*Fresh blueberries burst with flavor when cooked, and their sharpness complements
the rich flesh of mackerel very well.*

INGREDIENTS
*2 tablespoons all-purpose
flour
4 smoked mackerel
fillets
4 tablespoons unsalted butter
juice of ½ lemon
salt and freshly ground black
pepper*

FOR THE BLUEBERRY SAUCE
*1 pound blueberries
2 tablespoons sugar
1 tablespoon unsalted butter*

SERVES 4

1 Season the flour with salt and freshly ground black pepper. Coat each fish fillet in the flour, covering it well.

2 Brush the fillets with butter and cook on a medium grill for a few minutes, until they are heated through and have a crisp coating.

3 To make the sauce, place the blueberries, sugar, butter and salt and pepper to taste in a small roasting pan and cook on the grill, stirring occasionally, for about 10 minutes. Serve immediately, drizzling the lemon juice over the mackerel and with the blueberries on the side.

MACKEREL WITH TOMATOES, PESTO AND ONION

· · ·

*Rich, oily fish like mackerel needs a sharp, fresh-tasting sauce to go with it;
this aromatic pesto is excellent drizzled over the top.*

INGREDIENTS

4 mackerel, cleaned and gutted
2 tablespoons olive oil
4 ounces onion, roughly chopped
*1 pound tomatoes, roughly
chopped*
*salt and freshly ground
black pepper*

FOR THE PESTO
2 ounces pine nuts
2 tablespoons fresh basil leaves
2 garlic cloves, crushed
*2 tablespoons freshly grated
Parmesan cheese*
2/3 cup extra virgin olive oil

SERVES 4

1 To make the pesto, place the pine
nuts, fresh basil leaves and garlic in a
food processor and blend to a rough
paste. Add the Parmesan and, with the
motor running, gradually add the oil.

2 Season the mackerel with plenty of
salt and freshly ground black pepper
and cook on a medium-hot grill for
12–15 minutes, turning once.

3 Meanwhile, heat the olive oil
in a large, heavy saucepan and sauté
the chopped onions until soft and
golden brown.

4 Stir the chopped tomatoes into the
contents of the saucepan and cook for
5 minutes. Serve the fish on top of the
tomato mixture and top with a
generous spoonful of the pesto.

117

CHARBROILED TUNA WITH FIERY PEPPER PUREE

Tuna is an oily fish that grills well and is meaty enough to combine successfully with strong flavors—even hot chili, as in this red pepper purée, which is excellent served with crusty bread.

INGREDIENTS

4 tuna steaks, about 6 ounces each
finely grated rind and juice of 1 lime
2 tablespoons olive oil
salt and freshly ground black pepper
lime wedges and crusty bread, to serve

FOR THE PEPPER PURÉE
2 red bell peppers, halved
3 tablespoons olive oil, plus extra
for brushing
1 small onion
2 garlic cloves, crushed
2 fresh red chilies
1 slice white bread without crusts,
diced
salt

SERVES 4

1 Trim any skin from the tuna and place the steaks in a single layer in a wide dish. Sprinkle with the lime rind and juice, olive oil, salt and black pepper. Cover with plastic wrap and chill in the refrigerator until needed.

Cook's Tip

The pepper purée can be made ahead: cook the peppers and onion under a hot broiler and refrigerate them until you cook the fish.

2 To make the pepper purée, brush the pepper halves with a little olive oil and cook them, skin side down, on a hot grill, until the skin is charred and blackened. Place the onion in its skin on the grill and cook until browned, turning it occasionally.

3 Set aside the peppers and onion until cool enough to handle, then remove the skins, using a sharp knife.

4 Place the cooked peppers and onion with the garlic, chilies, bread and olive oil in a food processor. Process until smooth. Add salt to taste.

5 Drain the tuna steaks from the marinade and cook them on a hot grill for 8–10 minutes, turning once, until golden brown. Serve the steaks with the pepper purée and lime wedges, and crusty bread if desired.

TROUT WITH BACON

• • •

*The smoky, savory flavor of crisp grilled bacon perfectly complements
the delicate flesh of the trout in this simple dish.*

INGREDIENTS

4 trout, cleaned and gutted
1 tablespoon all-purpose flour
4 slices lean smoked bacon
2 tablespoons olive oil
juice of ½ lemon
salt and freshly ground
black pepper

SERVES 4

1 Place the trout on a chopping
board and pat dry with paper towels.
Season the flour with the salt and
freshly ground black pepper. Stretch
the bacon slices out thinly using the
back of a heavy kitchen knife.

2 Roll the fish in the seasoned flour
mixture and wrap tightly in the bacon
slices. Brush with olive oil and cook on
a medium-hot grill for 10–15 minutes,
turning once. Serve at once, with the
lemon juice drizzled on top.

RED MULLET WITH BASIL AND CITRUS

• • •

This Italian recipe is full of the warm, distinctive flavors of the Mediterranean.
Serve the dish with plain boiled rice and a green salad, or with lots of fresh crusty bread.

INGREDIENTS

4 red mullet, about 8 ounces each,
filleted
4 tablespoons olive oil
10 peppercorns, crushed
2 oranges, one peeled and sliced
and one squeezed
1 lemon
1 tablespoon butter
2 drained canned anchovies,
chopped
4 tablespoons shredded fresh basil
salt and freshly ground black
pepper

SERVES 4

1 Place the fish fillets in a shallow dish in a single layer. Pour the olive oil over them and sprinkle with the crushed peppercorns. Lay the orange slices on top of the fish. Cover the dish with plastic wrap and marinate in the refrigerator for at least 4 hours.

2 Halve the lemon. Remove the skin and pith from one half using a small, sharp knife, and slice the flesh thinly. Squeeze the juice from the other half.

3 Drain the fish, reserving the marinade and orange slices, and cook on a medium-hot grill for 10–12 minutes, turning once and basting with the marinade.

4 Melt the butter in a saucepan with any remaining marinade. Add the chopped anchovies and cook until completely soft. Stir in the orange and lemon juice and allow to simmer on the edge of the grill until slightly reduced. Stir in the basil and check the seasoning. Pour the sauce over the fish and garnish with the reserved orange slices and the lemon slices.

FISH PARCELS

. . .

*Sea bass is good for this recipe, but you could also use small whole trout
or a white fish fillet such as cod or haddock.*

INGREDIENTS

*4 pieces sea bass fillet, or 4 small
sea bass, about 1 pound each
olive oil for brushing
2 shallots, thinly sliced
1 garlic clove, chopped
1 tablespoon capers
6 sun-dried tomatoes, finely
chopped
4 black olives, pitted and thinly
sliced
grated rind and juice of 1 lemon
1 teaspoon paprika
salt and freshly ground black
pepper*

SERVES 4

1 Clean the fish if whole. Cut 4
squares of aluminum foil, large enough
to enclose the fish; brush lightly with a
little olive oil.

2 Place a piece of fish in the center
of each piece of foil and season well
with plenty of salt and pepper.

3 Sprinkle the shallots, chopped
garlic, capers, tomatoes, sliced olives
and lemon rind over the fish. Sprinkle
with the lemon juice and paprika.

4 Fold over the foil to enclose
the fish loosely, sealing the edges firmly
so that none of the juices can escape
during cooking. Place the parcels
on a moderately hot grill and cook
for 8–10 minutes. To serve, place each
of the parcels on a plate and loosen
the top to open.

Cook's Tip

These parcels can also
be baked in the oven: Place
them on a baking sheet and
cook at 400°F for 15 to
20 minutes.

SPICED FISH BAKED THAI STYLE

• • •

Banana leaves make a perfect, natural wrapping for grilled foods, but if they are not available you can use aluminum foil instead.

INGREDIENTS

4 red snapper or mullet, about
12 ounces each
banana leaves
1 lime
1 garlic clove, thinly sliced
2 scallions, thinly sliced
2 tablespoons Thai red
curry paste
4 tablespoons coconut milk

SERVES 4

1 Clean the fish, removing the scales, and make several deep slashes in the side of each one with a sharp knife. Place each fish on a layer of banana leaves.

2 Thinly slice half the lime and tuck the slices into the slashes in the fish, with the slivers of garlic. Sprinkle the sliced scallions over the fish.

3 Grate the rind and squeeze the juice from the remaining lime half and mix with the curry paste and coconut milk. Spoon over the fish.

4 Wrap the leaves over the fish, enclosing them completely. Tie firmly with string and cook on a medium-hot grill for 15–20 minutes, turning occasionally. To serve, open up the parcels by cutting along the top edge with a knife and fanning out the leaves.

SEA BREAM WITH ORANGE BUTTER SAUCE
. . .

Sea bream is a revelation to anyone unfamiliar with its creamy rich flavor.
The fish has a firm white flesh that goes well with this rich butter sauce, sharpened with orange.

INGREDIENTS
2 sea bream, about 12 ounces each,
scaled and gutted
2 teaspoons Dijon mustard
1 teaspoon fennel seeds
2 tablespoons olive oil, plus extra
for brushing
2 ounces watercress
6 ounces mixed lettuce leaves

FOR THE ORANGE BUTTER SAUCE
2 tablespoons frozen orange juice
concentrate
12 tablespoons (1½ sticks) unsalted
butter, diced
salt and cayenne pepper

SERVES 2

1 Slash the fish 4 times on each side.
Combine the mustard and fennel seeds,
then spread on both sides of the fish.
Brush with olive oil and cook on a
medium-hot grill for 10–12 minutes,
turning once.

2 Place the orange juice concentrate
in a bowl and heat over a saucepan of
simmering water. Remove the pan from
the heat and gradually whisk in the
butter until creamy. Season well.

3 Dress the watercress and lettuce
leaves with the remaining olive oil,
and arrange with the fish on two plates.
Spoon the sauce over the fish and serve
with baked potatoes, if desired.

HALIBUT WITH FRESH TOMATO AND BASIL SALSA

Take care when cooking this dish, as halibut has a tendency to break easily, especially when the skin has been removed. Season well to bring out the flavor of the fish and the taste of the sauce.

INGREDIENTS

4 halibut fillets, about 6 ounces
each
3 tablespoons olive oil

FOR THE SALSA
1 medium tomato, roughly
chopped
¼ red onion, finely chopped
1 small jalapeño pepper
2 tablespoons balsamic vinegar
10 large fresh basil leaves
1 tablespoon olive oil
salt and freshly ground black
pepper

SERVES 4

1 To make the salsa, mix together the chopped tomato, red onion, jalapeño pepper and balsamic vinegar in a bowl. Slice the fresh basil leaves finely, using a sharp kitchen knife.

2 Stir the basil and the olive oil into the tomato mixture. Season to taste. Cover the bowl with plastic wrap and let sit for at least 3 hours.

3 Rub the halibut fillets with oil and season them. Cook on a medium grill for 8 minutes, basting with oil and turning once. Serve with the salsa.

COD FILLETS WITH FRESH MIXED-HERB CRUST

• • •

Use fresh herbs and whole-wheat bread crumbs to make a delicious coating for the fish.
Season the fish well and serve with large lemon wedges.

INGREDIENTS

2 tablespoons butter
4 thick pieces of cod fillet, about
8 ounces each, skinned
3 cups whole-wheat bread crumbs
1 tablespoon each finely chopped
fresh chervil, chives and parsley,
plus extra, to garnish
1 tablespoon olive oil
lemon wedges, to garnish
salt and freshly ground black
pepper

SERVES 4

1 Melt the butter and use some of it to brush onto the cod fillets. Mix any remaining melted butter with the whole-wheat bread crumbs and finely chopped fresh herbs. Season with plenty of salt and freshly ground black pepper.

2 Press a quarter of the mixture onto each fillet, spreading evenly, and lightly sprinkle with olive oil. Cook on a medium grill for about 10 minutes, turning once. Serve the fish garnished with lemon wedges and sprigs of fresh herbs.

GRILLED SNAPPER WITH HOT MANGO SALSA

• • •

A ripe mango provides the basis for a deliciously rich fruity salsa that needs no oil and features the tropical flavors of cilantro, ginger and chilies.

INGREDIENTS

12 ounces new potatoes

3 eggs

4 ounces young green beans,
trimmed and halved

4 red snapper, about 12 ounces
each, cleaned, scaled and gutted

2 tablespoons olive oil, plus extra
for brushing

6 ounces mixed lettuce leaves

2 cherry tomatoes

salt and freshly ground black
pepper

FOR THE SALSA

3 tablespoons chopped fresh cilantro

1 medium-size ripe mango, peeled,
pitted and diced

½ fresh red chili, seeded and
chopped

1-inch piece fresh ginger, grated

juice of 2 limes

generous pinch of celery salt

SERVES 4

1 Place the potatoes in a large saucepan of salted water. Bring to a boil and simmer for 15–20 minutes· drain.

2 Bring a second large saucepan of salted water to a boil. Put in the eggs and boil for 4 minutes, then add the beans and cook for another 6 minutes, so that the eggs have had a total of 10 minutes. Remove the eggs from the saucepan. Drain and refresh the beans. Cool, then shell the eggs and cut into quarters.

3 Using a sharp knife, slash each snapper 3 times on each side. Brush with olive oil and cook on a medium-hot grill for 12 minutes, basting occasionally and turning once.

4 To make the salsa, place the chopped fresh cilantro in a food processor. Add the mango chunks, chili, grated ginger, lime juice and celery salt and process until smooth.

5 Dress the lettuce leaves with olive oil and distribute them evenly among four large plates.

6 Arrange the snapper on the lettuce and season to taste. Halve the new potatoes and distribute them with the beans, tomatoes and quartered hard-boiled eggs over the salad. Serve immediately, with the salsa.

Variation

If fresh mangoes are unavailable, use canned ones, draining well. Sea bream are also good served with this hot mango salsa.

SMOKED HADDOCK WITH QUICK PARSLEY SAUCE

· · ·

Make any herb sauce by this method, making sure it is thickened and seasoned well to complement the smoky flavor of the fish.

INGREDIENTS

4 smoked haddock fillets, about
8 ounces each
6 tablespoons butter, softened
2 tablespoons all-purpose flour
1¼ cups milk
4 tablespoons chopped fresh parsley
salt and freshly ground black
pepper

SERVES 4

1 Smear the fish fillets on both sides with 4 tablespoons of the butter.

2 Beat the remaining butter and the flour together to make a paste.

3 Cook the fish on a medium-hot grill for about 10 minutes, turning once. Meanwhile, to make the sauce, heat the milk in a saucepan to just below boiling point. Add the flour mixture in small spoonfuls, whisking constantly over the heat. Continue until the sauce is smooth and thick.

4 Add the seasoning and chopped fresh parsley to the saucepan and stir well. Pour the parsley sauce over the haddock fillets to serve.

SALMON WITH RED ONION MARMALADE

. . .

Salmon grills well but is most successful when it is at least an inch thick. The red onion marmalade is rich and delicious. Puréed black currants work as well as crème de cassis.

INGREDIENTS

4 salmon steaks, about 6 ounces
each
2 tablespoons olive oil
salt and freshly ground black
pepper

FOR THE RED ONION MARMALADE
5 medium red onions, peeled and
finely sliced
4 tablespoons butter
3/4 cup red wine vinegar
1/4 cup crème de cassis
1/4 cup grenadine
1/4 cup red wine

SERVES 4

1 Use your hands to rub the olive oil into the salmon flesh and season with plenty of salt and freshly ground black pepper.

2 Melt the butter in a large, heavy saucepan and add the sliced onions. Sauté the onions for 5 minutes, until golden brown.

3 Stir in the vinegar, crème de cassis, grenadine and wine and continue to cook for about 10 minutes, until the liquid has almost entirely evaporated and the onions are glazed. Season well.

4 Brush the fish with a little more oil and cook on a medium grill for 6–8 minutes, turning once.

131

GRILLED SEA BASS WITH CITRUS FRUIT

• • •

*Sea bass is a beautiful fish with a soft, dense texture and a delicate flavor. In this recipe
it is complemented by citrus fruits and fruity olive oil.*

INGREDIENTS

1 small grapefruit
1 orange
1 lemon
1 sea bass, 3–3½ pounds, cleaned
and scaled
6 fresh basil sprigs
1 tablespoon olive oil, plus extra
for brushing
4–6 shallots, halved
4 tablespoons dry white wine
1 tablespoon butter
salt and freshly ground black
pepper
fresh dill, to garnish

SERVES 6

1 Using a vegetable peeler, remove the rind from the grapefruit, orange and lemon. Cut into thin julienne strips. Peel the pith from the fruits and, working over a bowl to catch the juices, cut out the segments from the grapefruit and the orange and set aside for the garnish. Slice the lemon thickly.

2 Season the cavity of the fish with salt and pepper and slash the flesh 3 times on each side. Reserving a few basil sprigs for the garnish, fill the cavity with the remaining basil, the lemon slices and half the julienne strips of citrus rind. Brush with olive oil and cook on a medium-low grill for about 20 minutes, basting occasionally and turning once.

3 Meanwhile, heat 1 tablespoon olive oil in a pan and cook the shallots gently until soft. Add the wine and 2–3 tablespoons of the fruit juice to the pan. Bring to a boil over high heat, stirring. Stir in the remaining julienne strips of rind and boil for 2–3 minutes, then whisk in the butter.

4 When the fish is cooked, transfer it to a serving dish. Remove and discard the stuffing. Spoon the shallots and sauce around the fish and garnish with fresh dill sprigs, the reserved basil and segments of grapefruit and orange.

GRILLED SEA BASS WITH FENNEL

• • •

The classic combination of sea bass and fennel works particularly well when the fish is cooked over charcoal. Traditionally, fennel twigs are used, but this version of the dish uses fennel seeds.

INGREDIENTS

1 sea bass, 3–3 ½ pounds, cleaned and scaled
4 tablespoons olive oil
2 teaspoons fennel seeds
2 large fennel bulbs
4 tablespoons Pernod
salt and freshly ground black pepper

SERVES 6

1 Make 4 deep slashes in each side of the fish. Brush the fish with olive oil and season well with salt and freshly ground black pepper. Sprinkle the fennel seeds in the cavity and slashes of the fish. Cook on a low grill for 20 minutes, basting occasionally and turning once.

2 Meanwhile, trim and slice the fennel bulbs thinly, reserving any leafy fronds to use as a garnish. Brush the slices with olive oil and grill for 8–10 minutes, turning the fish occasionally, until tender. Remove the fish from the heat and keep it warm.

3 Scatter the fennel slices on a serving plate. Lay the fish on top and garnish with the reserved fennel fronds.

4 When ready to eat, heat the Pernod in a small pan on the side of the grill, light it and pour it, flaming, over the fish. Serve at once.

133

MEXICAN BARBECUED SALMON

○ ○ ○

The sauce for this dish is vibrant with hot, sweet and sour flavors
that permeate the fish before and during cooking.

INGREDIENTS

1 small red onion
1 garlic clove
6 plum tomatoes
2 tablespoons butter
3 tablespoons ketchup
2 tablespoons Dijon mustard
2 tablespoons dark brown sugar
1 tablespoon honey
1 tablespoon cayenne pepper
1 tablespoon ancho chili powder
1 tablespoon paprika
1 tablespoon Worcestershire sauce
4 salmon fillets, about 6 ounces
each

SERVES 4

3 Melt the butter in a large, heavy saucepan and gently cook the onion and garlic until translucent.

4 Add the tomatoes to the saucepan and allow to simmer for 15 minutes.

5 Add the remaining ingredients, excluding the salmon, and simmer for another 20 minutes. Pour the mixture into a food processor and blend until smooth. Set aside to cool.

1 Using a sharp knife, finely chop the red onion and finely dice the garlic.

6 Brush the salmon with the sauce, and chill for at least 2 hours. Cook on a hot grill for 6 minutes, basting with the sauce and turning once.

2 Next, dice the plum tomatoes finely and set them aside.

SALMON WITH TROPICAL FRUIT SALSA

. . .

Fresh salmon really needs little adornment, but it does combine very well with the exotic flavors in this colorful salsa.

INGREDIENTS

4 salmon steaks or fillets, about 6
ounces each
finely grated rind and juice of
1 lime
1 small, ripe mango
1 small, ripe papaya
1 fresh red chili
3 tablespoons chopped fresh
cilantro
salt and freshly ground black
pepper

SERVES 4

3 Halve the papaya, scoop out the seeds with a spoon and remove the peel. Finely chop the flesh and add it to the mango in the bowl.

5 Combine the mango, papaya, chili and cilantro in a bowl and stir in the remaining lime rind and juice. Season to taste with plenty of salt and freshly ground black pepper.

1 Place the salmon in a wide dish and sprinkle with half the lime rind and juice. Season with salt and pepper.

2 Cut the mango in half, cutting along each side of the pit; remove the pit. Finely chop the mango flesh and place it in a bowl.

4 Cut the chili in half lengthwise. Leave the seeds in to make the salsa hot and spicy, or remove them for a milder flavor. Finely chop the chili.

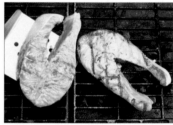

6 Cook the salmon on a medium grill for 5–8 minutes, turning once. Serve with the fruit salsa.

VEGETARIAN DISHES AND VEGETABLES

Vegetables cooked on the grill acquire a richness and depth of flavor

that will add an extra dimension to your meal. There are lots of ideas

here for vegetable accompaniments to meat and fish dishes, as well as

for substantial main dishes that everyone, vegetarian or not, will love.

All vegetables can be cooked in aluminum foil parcels, but many are

ideally suited to cooking on the grill: jacket potatoes, bell peppers,

eggplant and corn on the cob are irresistible cooked over charcoal, or

you can spear a mixture of vegetables onto skewers to make colorful

and delicious kebabs. Charbroiled vegetables can also be cooled and

made into fabulous salads. They certainly shouldn't be an afterthought

on your barbecue menu.

RED BEAN AND MUSHROOM BURGERS

· · ·

Vegetarians, vegans and meat-eaters alike will enjoy these healthy, low-fat veggie burgers.
With salad, pita bread and thick, creamy plain yogurt, they make a substantial meal.

INGREDIENTS

1 tablespoon olive oil
1 small onion, finely chopped
1 garlic clove, crushed
1 teaspoon ground cumin
1 teaspoon ground coriander
1/2 teaspoon ground turmeric
1 1/2 cups finely chopped
mushrooms
14-ounce can red kidney beans
2 tablespoons chopped fresh
cilantro
whole-wheat flour (optional)
olive oil, for brushing
salt and freshly ground black pepper
strained plain yogurt and
green salad, to serve

SERVES 4

2 Add the chopped mushrooms and cook, stirring, until softened and dry. Remove the pan from the heat and empty the contents into a large bowl.

3 Drain the beans thoroughly, place them in a bowl and mash with a fork.

4 Stir the kidney beans into the frying pan, with the chopped fresh cilantro, and mix thoroughly. Season the mixture with plenty of salt and freshly ground black pepper.

5 Using floured hands, form the mixture into 4 flat burger shapes. If the mixture is too sticky to handle, mix in a little whole-wheat flour.

6 Lightly brush the burgers with olive oil and cook on a hot grill for 8–10 minutes, turning once, until golden brown. Serve with a spoonful of yogurt and a green salad, if desired.

1 Heat the olive oil in a frying pan and fry the chopped onion and garlic over moderate heat, stirring, until softened. Add the spices and cook for a minute more, stirring constantly.

Cook's Tip

These burgers are not quite as firm as hamburgers, and will need careful handling on the grill.

GRILLED GOAT CHEESE PIZZA
· · ·

Pizzas cooked on the grill have a beautifully crisp and golden crust. The combination of goat cheese and red onion in this recipe makes for a flavorful main course dish.

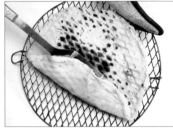

2 Brush the dough round with olive oil and place, oiled side down, on a medium grill. Cook for 6–8 minutes, until firm and golden underneath. Brush the uncooked side with olive oil and turn the pizza over.

3 Mix together the tomato sauce and pesto and quickly spread over the cooked side of the pizza, to within about ½ inch of the edge. Arrange the onion, tomatoes and cheese on top and sprinkle with salt and pepper.

INGREDIENTS

5-ounce package pizza-dough mix
olive oil, for brushing
⅔ cup tomato sauce
2 tablespoons tomato pesto
1 small red onion, thinly sliced
8 cherry tomatoes, halved
4 ounces firm goat cheese, thinly sliced
handful shredded fresh basil leaves
salt and freshly ground black pepper

SERVES 4

1 Make up the pizza dough according to the directions on the package. Roll out the dough on a lightly floured surface to a round about 10 inches in diameter.

4 Cook the pizza for 10 minutes more, until golden brown and crisp. Sprinkle with fresh basil and serve.

RED ONION GALETTES

○ ○ ○

*If non-vegetarians are going to eat these pretty puff pastry tarts, you can sprinkle some
chopped anchovies over them before grilling to add extra piquancy.*

INGREDIENTS

4–5 tablespoons olive oil
1¼ pounds red onions, sliced
1 garlic clove, crushed
2 tablespoons chopped fresh mixed
herbs, such as thyme, parsley and
basil
8 ounces ready-made puff pastry
1 tablespoon sun-dried tomato
paste
freshly ground black pepper
fresh thyme sprigs, to garnish

SERVES 4

1 Heat 2 tablespoons oil in a frying
pan and add the onions and garlic.
Cover and cook gently for 15–20
minutes, stirring occasionally, until soft
but not browned. Stir in the herbs.

2 Divide the pastry into 4 pieces and
roll out each piece to a 6-inch round.
Flute the edges, prick all over with a
fork and place on baking sheets.

3 Chill the rounds, on the baking
sheets, in the refrigerator for 10
minutes. Mix 1 tablespoon of the olive
oil with the sun-dried tomato paste and
spread over the pastry rounds, to
within about ½ inch of the edge.

4 Spread the onion mixture over
the pastry and season with pepper.
Drizzle with a little oil, then place the
baking sheets on a medium grill for
15 minutes, until the pastry is crisp.
Serve hot, garnished with thyme sprigs.

TOFU SATAY

° ° °

Grill cubes of tofu until crisp, then serve with a Thai-style peanut sauce. Soak the satay sticks
before use to prevent them from burning while on the grill.

INGREDIENTS

7-ounce package smoked tofu
3 tablespoons light soy sauce
2 teaspoons sesame oil
1 garlic clove, crushed
1 yellow and 1 red bell pepper, cut
into squares
8–12 fresh bay leaves
sunflower oil, for brushing

FOR THE PEANUT SAUCE
2 scallions, finely chopped
2 garlic cloves, crushed
generous pinch of chili powder, or
a few drops of hot chili sauce
1 teaspoon sugar
1 tablespoon white wine vinegar
2 tablespoons light soy sauce
3 tablespoons crunchy peanut butter

SERVES 4–6

1 Cut the tofu into bite-size cubes
and place in a large bowl. Add the soy
sauce, sesame oil and crushed garlic
and mix well. Cover with plastic wrap
and marinate for at least 20 minutes.

2 Using a wooden spoon, beat all the
peanut sauce ingredients together in a
large bowl. Do not use a food
processor to blend the ingredients, as
the texture should be slightly chunky.

3 Drain the tofu and thread the cubes
onto 8–12 satay sticks, alternating the
tofu with the bell pepper squares and
bay leaves. Larger bay leaves may need
to be halved before threading.

4 Brush the satays with sunflower
oil and cook on a hot grill or under the
broiler, turning occasionally, until the
tofu and peppers are browned and
crisp. Serve hot with the peanut sauce.

SWEET AND SOUR VEGETABLES WITH PANEER

• • •

The Indian cheese used in this recipe, called paneer, can be bought at Asian stores, or you can use tofu in its place. Paneer has a good firm texture and cooks very well on the grill.

INGREDIENTS

1 green and 1 yellow bell pepper,
cut into squares
8 cherry, or 4 medium, tomatoes
8 cauliflower florets
8 fresh or canned pineapple chunks
8 cubes paneer

FOR THE SEASONED OIL
1 tablespoon soybean oil
2 tablespoons lemon juice
1 teaspoon salt
1 teaspoon freshly ground black
pepper
1 tablespoon honey
2 tablespoons chili sauce

SERVES 4

1 Thread the prepared vegetables, pineapple and paneer cubes onto 4 skewers, alternating the ingredients.

2 Mix together all the ingredients for the seasoned oil. If the mixture seems a little too thick, add 1 tablespoon water. Brush the vegetables with the seasoned oil.

3 Cook on a hot grill or under the broiler for 10 minutes, turning the skewers often and basting with the seasoned oil. Sprinkle with pepper and serve on a bed of plain boiled rice.

VEGETABLE KEBABS WITH PEPPERCORN SAUCE

° ° °

Vegetables invariably taste good when cooked on the grill. You can include other
vegetables in these kebabs, depending on what is available at the time.

INGREDIENTS

24 mushrooms
16 cherry tomatoes
16 large fresh basil leaves
2 zucchini, cut into 16 thick slices
16 large fresh mint leaves
1 large red bell pepper, cut into
16 squares

TO BASTE
8 tablespoons (1 stick) melted
butter
1 garlic clove, crushed
1 tablespoon crushed green
peppercorns
salt

FOR THE GREEN PEPPERCORN SAUCE
4 tablespoons butter
3 tablespoons brandy
1 cup heavy cream
1 teaspoon crushed green
peppercorns

SERVES 4

1 Thread the vegetables and herbs
onto 8 bamboo skewers that have been
soaked in water to prevent them from
burning: Place the fresh basil leaves
next to the tomatoes, and wrap the
mint leaves around the zucchini slices.

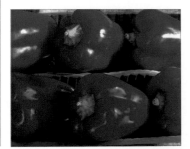

2 Mix the basting ingredients in a
bowl and baste the kebabs thoroughly.
Cook the skewers on a medium-hot
grill, turning and basting regularly,
until the vegetables are just cooked—
this should take 5–7 minutes.

3 Heat the butter for the green
peppercorn sauce in a frying pan,
then add the brandy and light it. When
the flames have died down, stir in the
cream and the peppercorns. Cook for
2 minutes, stirring constantly. Serve the
sauce with the grilled kebabs.

CASSAVA AND VEGETABLE KEBABS

• • •

This is an attractive and delicious assortment of African vegetables, marinated in a spicy garlic sauce, then roasted over hot coals. If cassava is unavailable, use sweet potato or yam instead.

INGREDIENTS

6 ounces cassava
1 onion, cut into wedges
1 eggplant, cut into bite-size pieces
1 zucchini, sliced
1 ripe plantain, sliced
1/2 red bell pepper and 1/2 green
bell pepper, sliced
16 cherry tomatoes
rice or couscous, to serve

FOR THE MARINADE
4 tablespoons lemon juice
4 tablespoons olive oil
3–4 tablespoons soy sauce
1 tablespoon tomato paste
1 green chili, seeded and finely
chopped
1/2 onion, grated
2 garlic cloves, crushed
1 teaspoon apple pie spice
pinch of dried thyme

SERVES 4

1 Peel the cassava and cut into bite-size pieces. Place in a large bowl, cover with boiling water and let it blanch for about 5 minutes. Drain well.

2 Place all the vegetables, including the cassava but not the tomatoes, in a large bowl and mix with your hands so that they are evenly distributed.

3 Blend the marinade ingredients in a bowl and pour over the vegetables. Cover and let marinate for 1–2 hours.

4 Thread the vegetables, with the cherry tomatoes, onto 8 skewers and cook on a hot grill for about 15 minutes, until tender and browned. Turn the skewers frequently and baste them occasionally with the marinade.

5 Pour the remaining marinade into a small saucepan and simmer for about 10 minutes to reduce. Strain the reduced marinade into a bowl. Serve the kebabs on a bed of rice or couscous, with the sauce on the side.

BAKED SQUASH WITH PARMESAN

• • •

Almost all types of squash are suitable for grilling, and they are extremely easy to deal with:
Simply wrap them in aluminum foil and place them in the hot embers until they soften.

INGREDIENTS

2 acorn or butternut squash,
about 1 pound each
1 tablespoon olive oil
4 tablespoons butter, melted
1 cup grated Parmesan cheese
4 tablespoons pine nuts, toasted
salt and freshly ground black
pepper
1/2 teaspoon freshly grated
nutmeg

SERVES 4

2 Brush the cut surfaces with oil and sprinkle with salt and black pepper.

3 Wrap each squash in foil and place in the embers of the fire. Cook for 25–30 minutes, until tender. Turn the parcels occasionally so that the squash cook evenly.

5 Dice the flesh, then stir in the melted butter. Add the Parmesan, pine nuts, salt and pepper. Toss well to mix.

6 Spoon the mixture back into the shells. Sprinkle with nutmeg to serve.

1 Cut the squash in half and scoop out the seeds with a spoon.

4 When they are cool enough to handle, unwrap the squash from the foil parcels and scoop out the flesh, leaving the skins intact.

Cook's Tip

Spaghetti squash can also be cooked in this way. Just scoop out the spaghetti-like strands and toss with butter and Parmesan cheese.

POTATO AND CHEESE POLPETTE

* * *

*These little morsels of potato and Greek feta cheese, flavored with dill and lemon juice,
are excellent when grilled, or they can be tossed in flour and fried in olive oil.*

INGREDIENTS

1¼ pounds potatoes
4 ounces feta cheese
4 scallions, chopped
3 tablespoons chopped fresh dill
1 egg, beaten
1 tablespoon lemon juice
2 tablespoons olive oil
*salt and freshly ground black
pepper*

SERVES 4

1 Boil the potatoes in their skins in
salted water until soft. Drain, then peel
while still warm. Place in a bowl and
mash. Crumble the feta cheese into the
potatoes and add the scallions, dill, egg
and lemon juice and season with
pepper and a little salt. Stir well.

2 Cover the mixture and chill until
firm. Divide the mixture into walnut-
size balls, then flatten them slightly.
Brush lightly with olive oil. Arrange
the polpette on a grill rack and cook on
a medium grill, turning once, until
golden brown. Serve at once.

LOOFAH AND EGGPLANT RATATOUILLE

Loofahs are edible gourds with spongy, creamy-white flesh. Their flavor, like that of eggplant, is intensified by roasting. Cooking the vegetables in a pan on the grill preserves their juices.

INGREDIENTS

1 large or 2 medium eggplants
1 pound young loofahs, or sponge
gourds
1 large red bell pepper, cut into
large chunks
8 ounces cherry tomatoes
8 ounces shallots
2 teaspoons ground coriander
4 tablespoons olive oil
2 garlic cloves, finely chopped
a few fresh cilantro sprigs
salt and freshly ground black
pepper

SERVES 4

1 Cut the eggplants into thick chunks and sprinkle the pieces liberally with salt to draw out the bitter juices. Allow to drain for about 45 minutes, then rinse under cold running water and pat dry with paper towels.

2 Slice the loofahs into ¾-inch pieces. Place the eggplant, loofah and pepper pieces, together with the cherry tomatoes and shallots, in a roasting pan large enough to hold all the vegetables in a single layer.

3 Sprinkle the vegetables with the ground coriander and olive oil. Sprinkle the chopped garlic and fresh cilantro leaves on top and season to taste.

4 Cook on the grill for about 25 minutes, stirring the vegetables occasionally, until the loofah is golden and the peppers are beginning to char. As an alternative, you could thread the vegetables on skewers and broil them.

BAKED STUFFED ZUCCHINI

• • •

The tangy goat cheese stuffing contrasts well with the very delicate flavor of the zucchini in this recipe. Wrap the zucchini in aluminum foil and bake them in the embers of the fire.

2 Insert pieces of goat cheese into the slits. Add a little chopped mint and sprinkle with the oil and black pepper.

3 Wrap each zucchini in foil, place in the embers of the fire and bake for about 25 minutes, until tender.

INGREDIENTS

8 small zucchini, about
1 pound total weight
1 tablespoon olive oil, plus
extra for brushing
3–4 ounces goat cheese,
cut into thin strips
a few sprigs of fresh mint,
finely chopped, plus extra
to garnish
freshly ground black pepper

SERVES 4

1 Cut 8 pieces of aluminum foil large enough to encase each zucchini and lightly brush with olive oil. Trim the zucchini and cut a thin slit along the length of each.

Cook's Tip

While almost any cheese can be used in this recipe, mild cheeses, such as Cheddar or mozzarella, will best allow the flavor of the zucchini to be appreciated.

VEGETABLE PARCELS WITH FLOWERY BUTTER

Nasturtium leaves and flowers are edible and have a distinctive peppery flavor.
They make a pretty addition to a summer barbecue.

INGREDIENTS

7 ounces baby carrots
9 ounces yellow pattypan squash
or summer squash
4 ounces baby corn
1 onion, thinly sliced
4 tablespoons butter, plus extra
for greasing
finely grated rind of ½ lemon
6 young nasturtium leaves
4–8 nasturtium flowers
salt and freshly ground
black pepper

SERVES 4

1 Trim the vegetables with a sharp knife, leaving them whole unless they are very large—if necessary, cut them into even-size pieces.

2 Divide the vegetables among 4 double-thickness squares of buttered aluminum foil and season well.

3 Mix the butter with the lemon rind in a small bowl. Roughly chop the nasturtium leaves and add them to the butter. Place a generous spoonful of the butter on each pile of vegetables in the squares of foil.

4 Fold over the foil and seal the edges to make a neat parcel. Cook on a medium-hot grill for 30 minutes, until the vegetables are tender. Open the parcels and top each with one or two nasturtium flowers. Serve at once.

GRILLED EGGPLANT PARCELS

These little bundles of tomatoes, mozzarella cheese and basil, wrapped in slices of eggplant, taste delicious cooked on the grill.

INGREDIENTS
2 large, long eggplants
8 ounces mozzarella cheese
2 plum tomatoes
16 large fresh basil leaves
2 tablespoons olive oil
salt and freshly ground black pepper

FOR THE DRESSING
4 tablespoons olive oil
1 teaspoon balsamic vinegar
1 tablespoon sun-dried tomato paste
1 tablespoon lemon juice

FOR THE GARNISH
2 tablespoons toasted pine nuts
torn fresh basil leaves

SERVES 4

3 Cut the mozzarella cheese into 8 slices. Cut each tomato into 8 slices, not counting the first and last slices. Take 2 eggplant slices and arrange in a cross. Place a slice of tomato in the center, season, then add a basil leaf, followed by a slice of mozzarella, another basil leaf, another slice of tomato and more seasoning.

4 Fold the ends of the eggplant slices around the filling to make a neat parcel. Repeat with the rest of the assembled ingredients to make 8 parcels. Chill the parcels in the refrigerator for about 20 minutes.

5 To make the tomato dressing, whisk together the olive oil, vinegar, sun-dried tomato paste and lemon juice. Season to taste with plenty of salt and freshly ground black pepper.

6 Brush the parcels with olive oil and cook on a hot grill for about 10 minutes, turning once, until golden. Serve hot, with the dressing, sprinkled with pine nuts and basil.

1 Remove the stalks from the eggplants and cut them lengthwise into thin slices using a mandoline or long-bladed knife—aim to get 16 slices total, each about ¼ inch thick, not counting the first and last slices.

2 Bring a large saucepan of salted water to the boil and cook the eggplant slices for about 2 minutes, until just softened. Drain the slices, then pat them dry on paper towels.

STUFFED TOMATOES AND PEPPERS

· · ·

Colorful peppers and tomatoes make perfect containers for meat and vegetable stuffings. The grilled flavors in this dish are simply superb.

INGREDIENTS

2 large ripe tomatoes
1 green bell pepper
1 yellow or orange bell pepper
4 tablespoons olive oil, plus extra
for sprinkling
2 onions, chopped
2 garlic cloves, crushed
1/2 cup blanched almonds, chopped
scant 1/2 cup long-grain rice, boiled
and drained
2 tablespoons roughly chopped
fresh mint
2 tablespoons roughly chopped
fresh parsley,
2 tablespoons golden raisins
3 tablespoons ground almonds
salt and freshly ground black
pepper
chopped mixed fresh herbs,
to garnish

SERVES 4

2 Halve the peppers, leaving the cores intact. Scoop out the seeds. Brush the peppers with 1 tablespoon olive oil and cook on a medium grill for 15 minutes. Place the peppers and tomatoes on a grill rack and season well with salt and pepper.

3 Fry the onions in the remaining olive oil for 5 minutes. Add the crushed garlic and chopped almonds to the pan and fry for a minute more.

4 Remove the pan from the heat and stir in the rice, chopped tomatoes, mint, parsley and golden raisins. Season well with salt and pepper and spoon the mixture into the tomatoes and peppers.

5 Sprinkle with the ground almonds and a little extra olive oil. Cook on a medium grill for about 15 minutes. Garnish with fresh herbs.

1 Cut the tomatoes in half and scoop out the pulp and seeds, using a teaspoon. Leave the tomatoes to drain on paper towels with the cut sides facing down. Roughly chop the tomato pulp and set it aside.

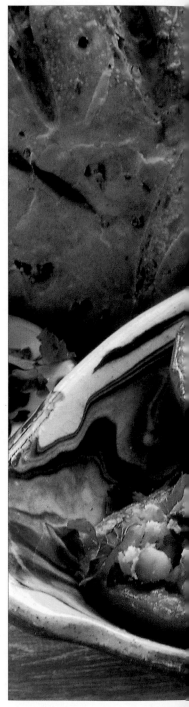

COUSCOUS-STUFFED PEPPERS

∘ ∘ ∘

Couscous makes a good basis for a stuffing, and in this recipe it is studded with raisins and flavored with fresh mint. Charred peppers make the combination of flavors truly special.

2 To cook the couscous, bring 1 cup water to a boil. Add the oil and salt, then remove from the heat and add the couscous. Stir and let stand, covered, for 5 minutes. Stir in the onion, raisins and mint. Season well and stir in the egg yolk.

3 Use a teaspoon to fill the peppers with the couscous mixture to about three-quarters full (the couscous will swell while cooking). Wrap each pepper in a piece of oiled aluminum foil.

4 Cook on a medium grill for 20 minutes, until tender. Serve hot or cool, garnished with mint leaves.

INGREDIENTS
6 red bell peppers
2 tablespoons butter
1 onion, finely chopped
1 teaspoon olive oil
1/2 teaspoon salt
1 cup couscous
2 tablespoons raisins
2 tablespoons chopped fresh mint
1 egg yolk
salt and freshly ground black pepper
mint leaves, to garnish

SERVES 4

1 Carefully slit each pepper with a sharp knife and remove the core and seeds. Melt the butter in a small saucepan and add the chopped onion. Cook until soft but not browned.

CORN ON THE COB IN A GARLIC BUTTER CRUST

• • •

Whether you are catering for vegetarians or serving this with meat dishes, it will disappear in a flash. The charred garlic butter crust adds a new dimension to the corn.

INGREDIENTS

6 ears of fresh corn
½ pound (2 sticks) butter
2 tablespoons olive oil
2 garlic cloves, crushed
1 cup whole-wheat bread crumbs
1 tablespoon chopped fresh
parsley
salt and freshly ground black
pepper

SERVES 6

1 Pull off the husks and silks and cook the corn in a large saucepan of boiling salted water until tender. Drain and set aside to cool.

2 Melt the butter in a saucepan, add the olive oil, crushed garlic, salt and freshly ground black pepper, and stir to blend. Pour the mixture into a shallow dish. In another shallow dish blend the bread crumbs and chopped fresh parsley. Roll the corn in the melted butter mixture and then in the bread crumbs until they are well coated.

3 Cook the corn on a hot grill for about 10 minutes, turning frequently, until the bread crumbs are golden brown.

STUFFED PARSLEYED ONIONS

· · ·

These stuffed onions are a popular vegetarian dish served with fresh crusty bread and a crisp salad. They also make a very good accompaniment to meat dishes.

INGREDIENTS

4 large onions
4 tablespoons cooked rice
4 teaspoons finely chopped fresh parsley, plus extra to garnish
4 tablespoons finely grated sharp Cheddar cheese
2 tablespoons olive oil
1 tablespoon white wine
salt and freshly ground black pepper

SERVES 4

1 Cut a slice from the top of each onion and scoop out the center, leaving a fairly thick shell. Combine all the remaining ingredients in a large bowl and stir to mix, moistening with enough white wine to bind the ingredients together well.

2 Use a spoon to fill the onions, then wrap each one in a piece of oiled aluminum foil. Bake in the embers of the fire for 30–40 minutes, until tender, turning the parcels often so they cook evenly. Serve the onions garnished with chopped fresh parsley.

STUFFED ARTICHOKE BOTTOMS

· · ·

The distinctive flavor of charbroiled globe artichokes is matched in this dish by an intensely savory stuffing of mushrooms, cheese and walnuts.

INGREDIENTS

8 ounces button mushrooms
1 tablespoon butter
2 shallots, finely chopped
2 ounces full- or medium-fat soft cheese, such as ricotta
2 tablespoons chopped walnuts
3 tablespoons grated Gruyère
4 large or 6 small artichoke bottoms (from cooked artichokes, leaves and choke removed, or cooked frozen or canned artichoke hearts)
salt and freshly ground black pepper
fresh parsley sprigs, to garnish

SERVES 4

1 To make the duxelles for the stuffing, put the mushrooms in a food processor or blender and pulse until finely chopped.

2 Melt the butter in a frying pan and cook the shallots over medium heat for 2–3 minutes, until just softened. Add the mushrooms, raise the heat slightly, and cook for 5–7 minutes more, stirring frequently, until all the liquid from the mushrooms has been driven off and they are almost dry. Season with plenty of salt and freshly ground black pepper.

3 In a large bowl, combine the soft cheese and cooked mushrooms. Add the chopped walnuts and half the grated Gruyère, and stir well to combine the mixture.

4 Arrange the artichoke bottoms in an oiled baking pan; divide the stuffing mixture among them. Sprinkle with the remaining grated cheese. Grill for 12 minutes, garnish with parsley and serve.

SPINACH WITH RAISINS AND PINE NUTS

• • •

Raisins and pine nuts are frequent partners in Spanish dishes. In this recipe, they are tossed with wilted spinach and croutons; the mixture can be cooked quickly in a flameproof pan on the grill.

INGREDIENTS

1/3 cup raisins
1 thick slice crusty white bread
3 tablespoons olive oil
1/3 cup pine nuts
1 1/4 pounds young spinach, stalks removed
2 garlic cloves, crushed
salt and freshly ground black pepper

SERVES 4

1 Put the raisins in a bowl, cover with boiling water and let soak for 10 minutes. Drain and set aside.

2 Cut the bread into cubes and discard the crusts. Heat 2 tablespoons of the olive oil in a large frying pan and fry the bread until golden brown.

3 Heat the remaining oil and fry the pine nuts, on the grill or stove, until beginning to color. Add the spinach and garlic and cook quickly, turning the spinach until it has just wilted. Toss in the raisins and season lightly with salt and pepper. Transfer to a serving dish. Scatter with croutons and serve.

GRILLED VEGETABLE TERRINE

* * *

A colorful layered terrine, using all the vegetables associated with the Mediterranean, makes a successful and elegant dish for outdoor eating. Grilling the vegetables adds to the flavor.

INGREDIENTS

*2 large red bell peppers,
quartered, cored and seeded
2 large yellow bell peppers,
quartered, cored and seeded
1 large eggplant, sliced
lengthwise
2 large zucchini, sliced
lengthwise
6 tablespoons olive oil
1 large red onion, thinly sliced
1/2 cup raisins
1 tablespoon tomato paste
1 tablespoon red wine vinegar
1 2/3 cups tomato juice
2 tablespoons powdered gelatin
fresh basil leaves, to garnish*

FOR THE DRESSING
*6 tablespoons extra virgin olive oil
2 tablespoons red wine vinegar
salt and freshly ground black
pepper*

SERVES 6

1 Cook the peppers, skin side down, on a hot grill or under the broiler, until the skins are beginning to blacken. Transfer to a bowl, cover and let cool.

2 Brush the eggplant and zucchini slices with oil and cook until tender and golden, turning occasionally.

3 Heat the remaining oil in a pan and add the onion, raisins, tomato paste and red wine vinegar. Cook until soft and syrupy. Allow to cool in the pan.

4 Pour half the tomato juice into a saucepan and sprinkle with the gelatin. Dissolve gently over very low heat, stirring constantly.

5 Line an oiled 7½-cup terrine with plastic wrap, leaving a little hanging over the sides. Place a layer of red peppers in the bottom and pour in enough of the tomato juice with gelatin to cover. Repeat with the eggplant, zucchini, yellow peppers and onion mixture, ending with another layer of red peppers and covering each layer with tomato juice and gelatin.

6 Add the remaining tomato juice to any left in the pan and pour into the terrine. Give it a sharp tap to eliminate air bubbles. Cover the terrine with plastic wrap and chill until set.

7 To make the dressing, whisk the oil and vinegar, and season with salt and black pepper. Turn out the terrine and serve in thick slices, drizzled with the dressing. Garnish with the basil leaves.

SUMMER VEGETABLES WITH YOGURT PESTO

• • •

*Grilled vegetables make a meal on their own, or are delicious served as a
Mediterranean-style accompaniment to grilled meats and fish.*

INGREDIENTS

2 small eggplants
2 large zucchini
1 red bell pepper
1 yellow bell pepper
1 fennel bulb
1 red onion
olive oil, for brushing
salt and freshly ground black
pepper

FOR THE YOGURT PESTO
⅔ cup strained plain yogurt
3 tablespoons pesto

SERVES 4

2 Use a sharp kitchen knife to cut
the zucchini in half lengthwise. Cut
the peppers in half, removing the seeds
but leaving the stalks in place.

5 Arrange the vegetables on the hot
grill, brush generously with olive oil
and sprinkle with plenty of salt and
freshly ground black pepper.

1 Cut the eggplants into ½-inch
slices. Sprinkle with salt and let drain
for about 30 minutes. Rinse well in
cold running water and pat dry.

3 Slice the fennel bulb and the red
onion into thick wedges, using a sharp
kitchen knife.

6 Cook the vegetables until golden
brown and tender, turning occasionally.
The eggplants and peppers will take
6–8 minutes to cook, the zucchini,
onion and fennel 4–5 minutes. Serve
the vegetables as soon as they are
cooked, with the yogurt pesto.

4 Stir the yogurt and pesto lightly
together in a bowl, to make a marbled
sauce. Spoon the yogurt pesto into a
serving bowl and set aside.

Cook's Tip
Baby vegetables make
excellent candidates for grilling
whole; look for baby eggplants
and peppers, in particular. There's
no need to salt the eggplants
if they're small.

WILD RICE WITH VEGETABLES

· · ·

Wild rice makes a special accompaniment to grilled vegetables in a simple vinaigrette dressing.
This recipe can be served as a side dish, but it also makes a tasty meal on its own.

INGREDIENTS

1 cup wild and long-grain rice
mixture
1 large eggplant, thickly sliced
1 red, 1 yellow and 1 green bell
pepper, quartered, cored and seeded
2 red onions, sliced
8 ounces shiitake mushrooms
2 small zucchini, cut in half
lengthwise
olive oil, for brushing
2 tablespoons chopped fresh thyme

FOR THE DRESSING
6 tablespoons extra virgin olive oil
2 tablespoons balsamic vinegar
2 garlic cloves, crushed
salt and freshly ground black
pepper

SERVES 4

1 Put the wild and long-grain rice mixture in a pan of cold salted water. Bring to a boil, then reduce the heat, cover and cook gently for 30–40 minutes, until the grains are tender (or follow the cooking instructions on the package, if appropriate).

2 To make the dressing, mix together the olive oil, vinegar, crushed garlic and seasoning in a bowl or screw-top jar until well blended.

3 Arrange the vegetables on a rack. Brush with olive oil and cook on a hot grill or broil for 8–10 minutes, until tender and well browned, turning them occasionally and basting with oil.

4 Drain the rice and toss with half the dressing. Pour into a serving dish and arrange the grilled vegetables on top. Pour in the remaining dressing and sprinkle with the chopped fresh thyme.

POTATO SKEWERS WITH MUSTARD DIP

• • •

Potatoes cooked on the grill have a good flavor and crisp skin.
These skewers are served with a thick, garlic-rich dip.

INGREDIENTS

2¼ pounds small new potatoes
7 ounces shallots, halved
2 tablespoons olive oil
1 tablespoon sea salt

FOR THE MUSTARD DIP
4 garlic cloves, crushed
2 egg yolks
2 tablespoons lemon juice
1¼ cups extra virgin olive oil
2 teaspoons whole-grain mustard
salt and freshly ground black
pepper

SERVES 4

1 To make the mustard dip, place the garlic, egg yolks and lemon juice in a blender or food processor and process for a few seconds, until smooth.

2 With the motor running, add the oil until the mixture forms a thick cream. Add the mustard and season.

3 Parboil the potatoes in salted boiling water for about 5 minutes. Drain well and then thread them onto metal skewers with the shallots.

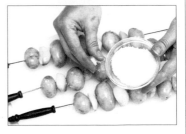

4 Brush with olive oil and sprinkle with sea salt. Cook for 10–12 minutes over a hot grill, turning often, until tender. Serve with the mustard dip.

POTATO WEDGES WITH GARLIC AND ROSEMARY

• • •

Toss the potato wedges in fragrant, garlicky olive oil with chopped fresh rosemary,
before grilling them over the coals.

INGREDIENTS

1½ pounds medium potatoes
1 tablespoon olive oil
2 garlic cloves, thinly sliced
4 tablespoons chopped fresh
rosemary
salt and freshly ground black
pepper

SERVES 4

1 Cut each potato into 4 wedges and parboil in boiling salted water for 5 minutes. Drain well.

2 Toss the potatoes in the olive oil with the garlic, rosemary and black pepper. Arrange on a grill rack.

3 Cook the potatoes on a hot grill for about 15 minutes, turning occasionally, until crisp and golden brown.

SPANISH POTATOES

This is an adaptation of a traditional recipe for peppery fried potatoes. Cook the potatoes in a flameproof dish on the grill or in a pan on the stove, and serve them with grilled meats.

INGREDIENTS

1½ pounds small new potatoes
5 tablespoons olive oil
2 garlic cloves, sliced
½ teaspoon crushed red pepper
½ teaspoon ground cumin
2 teaspoons paprika
2 tablespoons red or white wine
vinegar
1 red or green bell pepper, sliced
coarse sea salt, to serve (optional)

SERVES 4

1 Cook the potatoes in a saucepan of boiling salted water until almost tender. Drain and cut into chunks.

2 Heat the olive oil in a large frying pan or sauté pan and fry the potatoes, turning them frequently, until golden.

3 Meanwhile, crush the garlic, crushed red pepper and cumin in a mortar and pestle. Mix with the paprika and vinegar to form a thick paste.

4 Add the garlic mixture to the potatoes with the sliced bell pepper and cook, stirring, for 2 minutes. Serve warm or let sit until cool. Sprinkle with coarse sea salt, if you wish, to serve.

SALADS AND ACCOMPANIMENTS

———◆———

Cool salads are a perfect foil to grilled food, but they should

have assertive characters of their own. The recipes that follow

include some marvellous sunny, Mediterranean flavors that taste

especially good on summer days, and a selection of them would be

perfect as part of a buffet for a party. Don't forget that you can use

the grill to broil ingredients such as tomatoes, bell peppers, eggplant

and radicchio – it will give them an intense, smoky flavor that will

pervade the whole salad.

APPLE COLESLAW

. . .

There are many variations of this traditional salad; this recipe combines the sweet flavors of apple and carrot with a hint of celery. Prepare the salad in advance and chill until needed.

INGREDIENTS

1 pound white cabbage
1 medium onion
2 apples, peeled and cored
6 ounces carrots, peeled
²/₃ cup mayonnaise
1 teaspoon celery salt
freshly ground black pepper

SERVES 4

1 Remove the outer leaves from the cabbage and, using a heavy knife, cut it into 2-inch wedges. Remove and discard the stem sections.

2 Feed the cabbage wedges and the onion through the slicing blade of a food processor. Change to a grating blade and grate the apples and carrots. If you do not have a food processor, use a vegetable slicer and a hand grater.

3 Combine the salad ingredients in a large mixing bowl. Fold in the mayonnaise and season with celery salt and freshly ground black pepper. Garnish with apple slices and parsley.

Cook's Tip

This recipe can be adapted easily to suit different tastes. Add ½ cup chopped walnuts or raisins for added texture, or, for a richer, more substantial coleslaw, add ½ cup grated Cheddar cheese.

TOMATO AND FETA CHEESE SALAD

• • •

Sweet sun-ripened tomatoes are rarely more delicious than when mixed with feta cheese and olive oil. This salad can be served with any grilled meats, fish or vegetables.

INGREDIENTS

2 pounds tomatoes
7 ounces feta cheese
1/2 cup olive oil
12 black olives
4 sprigs fresh basil
freshly ground black pepper

SERVES 4

3 Crumble the feta cheese over the tomatoes, sprinkle with olive oil, then sprinkle with olives and fresh basil. Season with freshly ground black pepper and serve at room temperature.

1 Remove the tough cores from the tomatoes with a small kitchen knife.

2 Slice the tomatoes thickly on a chopping board and arrange the slices in a wide, shallow dish.

Cook's Tip

Feta cheese has a strong flavor and can be very salty. For an authentic flavor and texture, look for Greek, Cypriot or Turkish feta.

CURLY ENDIVE SALAD WITH BACON
• • •

When they are in season, young dandelion leaves could be included in this hearty French salad.
If you wish, sprinkle the salad with chopped hard-boiled egg.

2 Heat 1 tablespoon oil in a pan over medium heat and add the bacon. Fry until browned. Remove the bacon and drain on paper towels.

3 Add another 2 tablespoons oil to the pan and fry the bread cubes over medium heat, turning frequently, until browned. Remove the bread cubes with a slotted spoon and drain on paper towels. Discard any remaining fat.

INGREDIENTS

6 cups curly endive or escarole leaves
5–6 tablespoons extra virgin olive oil
6-ounce piece of smoked bacon, diced
thick slice of white bread, cubed
1 small garlic clove, finely chopped
1 tablespoon red wine vinegar
2 teaspoons Dijon mustard
salt and freshly ground black pepper

SERVES 4

1 Tear the lettuce leaves into bite-size pieces and put them in a large salad bowl. Set the bowl aside.

4 Stir the garlic, vinegar and mustard into the pan with the remaining oil and warm through. Season to taste. Pour the dressing over the salad and sprinkle with the fried bacon and croutons.

TABBOULEH

• • •

This classic Lebanese salad has become very popular everywhere. It makes an ideal substitute for a rice dish and is especially good with grilled lamb.

INGREDIENTS

1 cup fine bulgur
juice of 1 lemon
3 tablespoons olive oil
¾ cup chopped fresh parsley
3 tablespoons fresh mint, chopped
4–5 scallions, chopped
1 green bell pepper, sliced
salt and freshly ground black pepper
2 large tomatoes, diced, and black olives, to garnish

SERVES 4

1 Put the bulgur in a large bowl. Add enough cold water to cover and let it stand for at least 30 minutes and up to 2 hours.

2 Drain and squeeze the bulgur with your hands to remove excess water. The bulgur will swell to double its original size. Spread the bulgur evenly on paper towels to allow to dry completely.

3 Place the bulgur in a large bowl and add the lemon juice, the olive oil and a little salt and pepper. Allow to stand for 1–2 hours if possible, in order for the flavors to develop.

4 Add the chopped parsley, mint, scallions and pepper to the bowl and mix well. Garnish with diced tomatoes and olives and serve. The tabbouleh can be prepared in advance, covered with plastic wrap and stored in the refrigerator until needed.

PEPPERS WITH TOMATOES AND ANCHOVIES

• • ◦

This is a Sicilian-style salad full of warm Mediterranean flavors. The salad improves if it is made and dressed an hour or two before serving.

INGREDIENTS

1 red bell pepper
1 yellow bell pepper
4 ripe plum tomatoes, sliced
2 canned anchovies, drained and chopped
4 sun-dried tomatoes in oil, drained and sliced
1 tablespoon capers, drained
1 tablespoon pine nuts
1 garlic clove, very finely sliced

FOR THE DRESSING
5 tablespoons extra virgin olive oil
1 tablespoon balsamic vinegar
1 teaspoon lemon juice
chopped fresh mixed herbs
salt and freshly ground black pepper

SERVES 4

1 Cut the peppers in half and remove the seeds and stalks. Cut into quarters and cook, skin side down, over a hot grill or under the broiler until the skin chars. Transfer to a bowl and let cool. Peel the peppers and cut into strips.

2 Arrange the peppers and fresh tomatoes on a serving dish. Sprinkle the anchovies, sun-dried tomatoes, capers, pine nuts and garlic on top.

3 To make the dressing, mix together the olive oil, vinegar, lemon juice and chopped fresh herbs and season with plenty of salt and pepper. Pour the dressing over the salad before serving.

SWEET AND SOUR ONION SALAD

∘ ∘ ∘

This recipe for tangy glazed onions in the Provençal style makes an unusual and flavorful accompaniment to grilled steaks.

INGREDIENTS

1 pound baby onions, peeled
¼ cup wine vinegar
3 tablespoons olive oil
3 tablespoons sugar
3 tablespoons tomato paste
1 bay leaf
2 parsley sprigs
½ cup raisins
salt and freshly ground black pepper

SERVES 6

1 Put all the ingredients in a pan with 1¼ cups water. Bring to a boil and simmer gently, uncovered, for 45 minutes, or until the onions are tender and the liquid has evaporated.

2 Remove the bay leaf and parsley from the pan and check the seasoning. Transfer the contents of the pan to a large serving dish. Serve the salad at room temperature.

SPICED EGGPLANT SALAD

* * *

Serve this Middle Eastern–influenced salad with warm pita bread as an appetizer, or as an accompaniment to any number of grilled main-course dishes.

INGREDIENTS

2 small eggplants, sliced
5 tablespoons olive oil
1/4 cup red wine vinegar
2 garlic cloves, crushed
1 tablespoon lemon juice
1/2 teaspoon ground cumin
1/2 teaspoon ground coriander
1/2 cucumber, thinly sliced
2 ripe, flavorful tomatoes,
thinly sliced
2 tablespoons plain yogurt
salt and freshly ground black
pepper
chopped flat-leaf parsley, to
garnish

SERVES 4

1 Brush the eggplant slices lightly with some of the olive oil and cook over a hot grill or under the broiler until golden and tender, turning once. Allow the slices to cool slightly, then cut them into quarters.

2 Mix the remaining olive oil with the vinegar, crushed garlic, lemon juice, and ground cumin and coriander. Season with plenty of salt and pepper and mix thoroughly. Add the warm eggplant, stir well and chill for at least 2 hours. Add the cucumber and tomatoes. Transfer the salad to a serving dish and spoon the yogurt on top. Garnish with chopped parsley to serve.

RADICCHIO, ARTICHOKE AND WALNUT SALAD
• • •

The distinctive, earthy taste of Jerusalem artichokes makes a lovely contrast to the sharp freshness of radicchio and lemon. Serve warm or cold as an accompaniment to grilled meats.

INGREDIENTS

1 large head of radicchio or
5 ounces radicchio leaves
6 tablespoons walnut pieces
3 tablespoons walnut oil
1¼ pounds Jerusalem artichokes
grated rind and juice of
1 lemon
coarse sea salt and freshly ground
black pepper
flat-leaf parsley, to garnish

SERVES 4

1 If using a whole radicchio, cut it into 8-10 wedges. Place the wedges or leaves in a flameproof dish. Scatter on the walnuts, drizzle with oil and season. Broil for 2–3 minutes.

2 Peel the artichokes and cut up any large ones so that the pieces are all roughly the same size. Add to a pan of boiling salted water with half the lemon juice and cook for 5–7 minutes until tender. Drain.

3 Toss the artichokes into the salad with the remaining lemon juice and the grated rind. Season with coarse sea salt and ground black pepper. Broil until just beginning to brown and serve at once, garnished with torn pieces of flat leaf parsley.

WARM FAVA BEAN AND FETA SALAD

∘ ∘ ∘

This recipe is loosely based on a typical medley of fresh-tasting salad ingredients—
fava beans, tomatoes and feta cheese. It's lovely either warm or cold.

INGREDIENTS

2 pounds fresh fava beans, or
12 ounces frozen fava beans
4 tablespoons olive oil
6 ounces plum tomatoes, halved,
or quartered if large
4 garlic cloves, crushed
4 ounces firm feta cheese, cut into
chunks
3 tablespoons chopped fresh dill,
plus extra to garnish
12 black olives
salt and freshly ground black
pepper

SERVES 4–6

1 Shell the fava beans, then cook them in boiling, salted water until they are just tender. Drain and set aside.

2 Meanwhile, heat the olive oil in a heavy frying pan and add the tomatoes and garlic. Cook until the tomatoes are beginning to color.

3 Add the feta to the frying pan and toss the ingredients together for 1 minute. Mix with the drained beans, dill, olives and salt and pepper. Serve garnished with the chopped fresh dill.

GRILLED HALOUMI AND GRAPE SALAD

In the eastern Mediterranean, haloumi cheese is often served grilled or fried for breakfast or supper. In this recipe it's tossed with sweet, juicy grapes, which complement its distinctive flavor.

INGREDIENTS

5 ounces mixed green salad leaves
3 ounces seedless green grapes
3 ounces seedless black grapes
9 ounces haloumi cheese
2 tablespoons olive oil
fresh young thyme leaves or dill, to garnish

FOR THE DRESSING

4 tablespoons olive oil
1 tablespoon lemon juice
1/2 teaspoon sugar
1 tablespoon chopped fresh thyme or dill
salt and freshly ground black pepper

SERVES 4

1 To make the dressing, mix the olive oil, lemon juice and sugar together in a bowl. Season with plenty of salt and black pepper. Stir in the chopped fresh thyme or dill and set aside.

2 Toss together the mixed green salad leaves and the green and black grapes, then transfer to a large serving plate or salad bowl.

3 Slice the haloumi cheese. Brush the slices with olive oil and cook briefly over a medium grill, or pan-fry on the stove, until golden, turning once.

4 Arrange the cooked cheese on top of the salad. Pour the dressing over it and garnish with thyme or dill leaves.

CHORIZO IN OLIVE OIL

• • •

*Spanish chorizo sausage has a deliciously pungent taste. Frying chorizo with onions and olive oil
is one of the best ways of using it; you can also cook it on the grill, brushed with olive oil.*

INGREDIENTS

5 tablespoons extra virgin olive oil
12 ounces chorizo sausage, sliced
1 large onion, thinly sliced
flat leaf parsley, roughly chopped,
to garnish

SERVES 4

1 Heat the olive oil in a frying pan
and fry the chorizo over high heat until
beginning to color. Remove from the
pan with a slotted spoon.

2 Add the onion slices to the pan
and fry until golden. Return the
sausage slices to the pan for about
1 minute to heat through.

3 Pour the mixture into a shallow
serving dish and sprinkle with the
chopped flat leaf parsley. Serve
the chorizo on its own or as a side
dish, with warm crusty bread.

Variation

Chorizo is usually available
in large supermarkets and
delicatessens, but any other
similar spicy sausage can be
used as a substitute.

FAVA BEAN, MUSHROOM AND CHORIZO SALAD

This salad can be served as a first course or as part of a buffet menu. Prepare it a day in advance and store it in the refrigerator until needed.

INGREDIENTS

8 ounces shelled fava beans
6 ounces chorizo sausage
4 tablespoons extra virgin olive oil
8 ounces crimini mushrooms,
sliced
handful of fresh chives
salt and freshly ground black
pepper

SERVES 4

1 Cook the beans in a large saucepan of boiling, salted water until just tender. Drain and refresh under cold running water. If the beans are large, peel away the tough outer skins.

2 Remove the skin from the chorizo and cut it into small chunks. Heat the oil in a frying pan, add the chorizo and cook for 2 minutes. Empty into a bowl with the mushrooms, mix well and set aside to cool.

3 Chop half the chives and stir the beans and chopped chives into the mushroom mixture. Season to taste. Serve the salad at room temperature, garnished with the remaining chives.

185

BABY EGGPLANTS WITH RAISINS AND PINE NUTS

• • •

This is a recipe with an Italian influence, in a style that would have been familiar in Renaissance times. If possible, make it a day in advance, to allow the sweet and sour flavors to develop.

INGREDIENTS

12 baby eggplants, halved
1 cup extra virgin olive oil
juice of 1 lemon
2 tablespoons balsamic vinegar
3 cloves
1/3 cup pine nuts
2 tablespoons raisins
1 tablespoon sugar
1 bay leaf
large pinch of crushed red pepper
salt and freshly ground black pepper

SERVES 4

1 Brush the eggplants with olive oil and cook over a hot grill for about 10 minutes, until charred, turning once.

2 To make the dressing, combine the remaining olive oil with the lemon juice, vinegar, cloves, pine nuts, raisins, sugar and bay leaf. Add the red pepper, salt and pepper and mix well.

3 Place the hot eggplants in an earthenware or glass bowl and pour the dressing over them. Let cool, turning the eggplants once or twice. Serve the salad at room temperature.

SQUASH A LA GRECQUE

· · ·

This salad makes a wonderful side dish for almost any barbecue meal. Cook the baby squash until they are perfectly tender, so that they can fully absorb the delicious flavors of the dressing.

INGREDIENTS

6 ounces pattypan squash
1 cup white wine
juice of 2 lemons
sprig of fresh thyme
1 bay leaf
handful of fresh chervil, roughly
chopped
1/4 teaspoon coriander seeds,
crushed
5 tablespoons olive oil
salt and freshly ground black
pepper

SERVES 4

3 Reduce the liquid by boiling rapidly for 10 minutes. Strain it and pour it over the squash. Let sit until cool for the flavors to be absorbed.

1 Blanch the pattypan squash in boiling water for 3 minutes, drain, then refresh under cold running water.

2 Place the remaining ingredients in a pan, add 2/3 cup water and bring to a simmer. Add the squash and cook for 10 minutes, then remove it.

Salsas, Dips and Marinades

—◆—

The powerful flavors of grilled meat and fish call for spicy, lively

accompaniments. Chunky salsas are ideal, with their intriguing

combination of cool, crisp ingredients and fiery flavors. Tangy barbecue

sauce is a more traditional alternative that children adore. For a subtler

effect, melt a pat of butter flavored with herbs, garlic or anchovies over

a plainly grilled steak or fish. This chapter also includes some appetizing

dips to go with potato chips, bread sticks and crudités, and a selection

of delicious marinades suitable for a wide variety of meat and fish.

FRESH CORN SALSA

• • •

Serve this succulent salsa with grilled ham or pork, or with smoked meats. The charbroiled fresh corn makes the salsa particularly flavorful.

INGREDIENTS

2 ears of fresh corn
2 tablespoons melted butter
4 tomatoes
6 scallions, finely chopped
1 garlic clove, finely chopped
2 tablespoons lemon juice
2 tablespoons olive oil
red Tabasco sauce, to taste
salt and freshly ground black pepper

SERVES 4

3 Skewer the tomatoes and hold them over the grill or broil them for about 2 minutes, turning, until the skin splits and wrinkles. Slip off the skins and dice the flesh. Add to the corn with the scallions and chopped garlic.

4 Stir the lemon juice and olive oil together, adding Tabasco, salt and black pepper to taste. Pour mixture over the salsa, stir well, cover and set aside to marinate at room temperature for 1–2 hours before serving.

1 Remove the husks and silks from the corn. Brush with the melted butter and gently grill or broil for about 20 minutes, turning occasionally, until tender and charred.

2 To remove the kernels, stand each ear upright on a chopping board and use a large, heavy knife to slice down its length. Put the kernels in a mixing bowl.

BARBECUE SAUCE

· · ·

Brush this sauce liberally over chicken pieces, chops or kebabs before cooking on the grill, or serve as a hot or cold accompaniment to hot dogs and hamburgers.

INGREDIENTS

2 tablespoons vegetable oil
1 large onion, chopped
2 garlic cloves, crushed
14-ounce can tomatoes
2 tablespoons Worcestershire sauce
1 tablespoon white wine vinegar
3 tablespoons honey
1 teaspoon mustard powder
1/2 teaspoon chili seasoning or mild chili powder
salt and freshly ground black pepper

SERVES 4

3 Pour into a food processor or blender and process until smooth.

4 Press through a sieve if you like. Adjust the seasoning to taste.

1 Heat the vegetable oil in a large saucepan and fry the onions and garlic until soft and golden.

2 Stir in the remaining ingredients and simmer, uncovered, for 15–20 minutes, stirring occasionally. Remove the saucepan from the heat and allow to cool slightly.

GUACAMOLE
. . .

Nachos or tortilla chips are the classic accompaniments for this classic Mexican dip, but it also tastes great served on the side with burgers or kebabs.

INGREDIENTS

2 ripe avocados
2 red chilies, seeded
1 garlic clove
1 shallot
2 tablespoons olive oil, plus
extra to serve
juice of 1 lemon
salt
fresh flat leaf parsley, to garnish

SERVES 4

1 Halve the avocados, flick out the pits using the point of a sharp knife, and use a teaspoon to scoop the flesh into a large bowl.

2 Mash the flesh well, using a potato masher or a large fork, so that the avocado is a fairly smooth consistency.

3 Finely chop the chilies, garlic clove and shallot, then stir into the mashed avocado with the olive oil and lemon juice. Add salt to taste and mix well.

4 Spoon the mixture into a serving bowl. Drizzle on a little more olive oil and sprinkle with flat leaf parsley leaves. Guacamole will not keep for very long but can be prepared up to 8 hours in advance and stored in the refrigerator, sprinkled with lemon juice and covered with plastic wrap.

CARAMELIZED ONION RELISH

. . .

Slow, gentle cooking reduces the onions to a soft, sweet relish, which would make a tasty addition to many barbecue menus.

2 Heat the butter and oil together in a large saucepan. Add the onions and sugar and cook very gently for 30 minutes over low heat, stirring occasionally, until reduced to a soft rich brown caramelized mixture.

3 Roughly chop the capers and stir them into the caramelized onions. Allow to cool completely.

4 Stir in the chopped fresh parsley and add salt and pepper to taste. Cover with plastic wrap and chill in the refrigerator until ready to serve.

INGREDIENTS

3 large onions
4 tablespoons butter
2 tablespoons olive oil
2 tablespoons light brown sugar
2 tablespoons capers
2 tablespoons chopped fresh parsley
salt and freshly ground black pepper

SERVES 4

1 Peel the onions and halve them vertically through the core, using a sharp knife. Slice them thinly.

PARSLEY BUTTER

• • •

This butter, or one of the variations below, makes a subtle accompaniment to grilled food, particularly fish with a delicate flavor.

INGREDIENTS

8 tablespoons softened butter
2 tablespoons finely chopped parsley
½ teaspoon lemon juice
cayenne pepper
salt and freshly ground black pepper

SERVES 4

1 Beat the butter until creamy, then beat in the parsley, lemon juice and cayenne pepper, and season lightly.

2 Spread the butter ¼ inch thick onto a piece of foil, chill, then cut into shapes with a knife or cookie cutter.

3 Alternatively, form the butter into a roll, wrap in plastic wrap or foil and chill. Cut off slices as required.

Variations

LEMON OR LIME BUTTER
Add 1 tablespoon finely grated lemon or lime rind and 1 tablespoon juice to the butter.

HERB BUTTER
Replace the parsley with 2 tablespoons chopped mint, chives or tarragon.

GARLIC BUTTER
Add 2 crushed garlic cloves to the butter with 1–2 tablespoons chopped parsley.

ANCHOVY BUTTER
Add 6 anchovy fillets, drained of oil and mashed with a fork, to the butter. Season with pepper only.

MUSTARD BUTTER
Add 2 teaspoons English mustard and 2 tablespoons chopped chives to the butter.

These butters will keep in the refrigerator for several days, and will also freeze well, wrapped in plastic wrap or foil to prevent any loss of flavor.

BASIL AND LEMON MAYONNAISE

• • •

This fresh mayonnaise is flavored with lemon and two types of basil. Serve as a dip with potato chips or crudités, or with salads and baked potatoes.

INGREDIENTS

2 egg yolks
1 tablespoon lemon juice
²/₃ cup olive oil
²/₃ cup sunflower oil
handful of green basil leaves
handful of opal basil leaves
4 garlic cloves, crushed
salt and freshly ground black pepper

SERVES 4

1 Place the egg yolks and lemon juice in a blender or food processor and process them briefly together.

2 In a pitcher, stir the oils together. With the machine running, pour in the oil very slowly, a drop at a time.

3 Once half the oil has been added, the remainder can be incorporated more quickly. Continue processing to form a thick, creamy mayonnaise.

4 Tear both types of basil into small pieces and stir into the mayonnaise with the crushed garlic and seasoning. Transfer to a serving dish, cover and chill until ready to serve.

MELLOW GARLIC DIP

• • •

Two whole heads of garlic may seem like too much, but, once they're cooked, the taste is sweet and mellow. Serve with crunchy breadsticks and potato chips.

2 When cool enough to handle, separate the garlic cloves and peel them. Place on a chopping board and sprinkle with salt. Mash the garlic with a fork until puréed.

3 Place the garlic in a large bowl and stir in the mayonnaise, yogurt and whole-grain mustard. Mix well.

INGREDIENTS

2 whole garlic heads
1 tablespoon olive oil
4 tablespoons mayonnaise
5 tablespoons strained plain yogurt
1 teaspoon whole-grain mustard
salt and freshly ground black pepper

SERVES 4

1 Slice the tops from the heads of garlic, using a sharp knife. Brush with olive oil and wrap in foil. Cook on a medium-hot grill or oven-broil for 25 minutes, turning occasionally.

4 Check the seasoning, adding more salt and pepper to taste, then spoon the dip into a serving bowl. Cover and chill in the refrigerator until ready to serve.

199

CREAMY EGGPLANT DIP

• • •

Spread this velvet-textured dip thickly on slices of French bread toasted on the grill, then top with slivers of sun-dried tomato to make wonderful Italian-style crostini.

INGREDIENTS

1 large eggplant
2 tablespoons olive oil
1 small onion, finely chopped
2 garlic cloves, finely chopped
4 tablespoons chopped fresh parsley
5 tablespoons crème fraîche
red Tabasco sauce, to taste
juice of 1 lemon, to taste
salt and freshly ground black
pepper

SERVES 4

3 Peel the eggplant and mash the flesh with a large fork or potato masher to make a pulpy purée.

4 Stir in the onion and garlic, parsley and crème fraîche. Add Tabasco, lemon juice, and salt and pepper. Serve warm.

1 Cook the whole eggplant on a medium grill or broil for about 20 minutes, turning occasionally, until the skin is blackened and the eggplant soft. Cover the eggplant with a clean dish towel and set aside to cool for about 5 minutes.

2 Heat the oil in a frying pan and cook the chopped onion and garlic for 5 minutes, until soft but not browned.

FAT-FREE SAFFRON DIP

. . .

Serve this mild dip with fresh vegetable crudités—it is particularly good with florets of cauliflower, asparagus tips and baby carrots and corn.

INGREDIENTS

1 tablespoon boiling water
small pinch saffron strands
scant 1 cup fat-free fromage frais
10 fresh chives
10 fresh basil leaves
salt and freshly ground black
pepper

SERVES 4

1 Pour the boiling water into a bowl and add the saffron strands. Allow to infuse for 3 minutes.

2 Beat the fromage frais in a large bowl until smooth. Stir in the infused saffron liquid with a wooden spoon.

Cook's Tip

If you don't have any saffron, add a squeeze of lemon or lime juice.

3 Snip the chives into the dip. Tear the basil leaves into small pieces and stir them in. Mix thoroughly.

4 Add salt and freshly ground black pepper to taste. Serve the dip with fresh vegetable crudités, if desired.

SPICY YOGURT MARINADE

· · ·

Use this marinade for chicken, lamb or pork, and marinate the meat, covered and chilled, for 24 to 36 hours to develop a mellow spicy flavor.

INGREDIENTS

1 teaspoon coriander seeds
2 teaspoons cumin seeds
6 cloves
2 bay leaves
1 onion, quartered
2 garlic cloves
2-inch piece fresh ginger, roughly
chopped
1/2 teaspoon chili powder
1 teaspoon ground turmeric
2/3 cup plain yogurt
juice of 1 lemon

SERVES 6

1 Spread the coriander and cumin seeds, cloves and bay leaves over the bottom of a large frying pan and dry-fry over moderate heat until the bay leaves are crisp.

2 Allow the spices to cool, then grind coarsely with a mortar and pestle.

3 Finely chop the onion, garlic and ginger in a blender or food processor. Add the ground spices, chili powder, turmeric, yogurt and lemon juice.

Cook's Tip
Garnish the finished dish with fresh cilantro leaves and slices of lemon or lime.

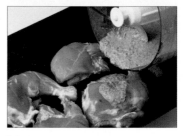

4 If you are marinating chicken parts or large pieces of meat, make several deep slashes to allow the flavors to penetrate. Arrange the pieces in a single layer and pour the marinade over them. Cover and place in the refrigerator to marinate for at least 24 hours.

ORANGE AND GREEN PEPPERCORN MARINADE

• • •

This is an excellent light marinade for delicately flavored whole fish such as sea trout,
bass or bream. The beauty of the fish is perfectly set off by the softly colored marinade.

INGREDIENTS

1 red onion
2 small oranges
6 tablespoons light olive oil
2 tablespoons cider vinegar
2 tablespoons green peppercorns in
brine, drained
2 tablespoons chopped fresh parsley
salt and sugar

FOR 1 MEDIUM-SIZE FISH

1 With a sharp knife, slash the fish
3 or 4 times on each side.

2 Cut a piece of foil big enough to
wrap the fish and use to line a large
dish. Peel and slice the onion and
oranges. Lay half the slices on the foil,
place the fish on top and cover with
the remaining onion and orange.

3 Mix the remaining marinade
ingredients and pour over the fish.
Cover and let marinate for 4 hours,
occasionally spooning the marinade
over the fish.

4 Fold the foil loosely over the fish
and seal the edges securely. Bake on
a medium grill for 15 minutes for
1 pound, plus 15 minutes more.

GINGER AND LIME MARINADE

· · ·

This fragrant marinade will guarantee a mouthwatering aroma from the grill. Shown here on shrimp and monkfish kebabs, it is just as delicious with chicken or pork.

INGREDIENTS

3 limes
1 tablespoon green cardamom
pods
1 onion, finely chopped
1-inch piece fresh ginger, grated
1 large garlic clove, crushed
3 tablespoons olive oil

SERVES 4–6

3 Mix all the marinade ingredients together and pour over the meat or fish. Stir gently, cover and set aside in a cool place to marinate for 2–3 hours.

4 Drain the meat or fish when you are ready to cook it on the grill. Baste the meat occasionally with the marinade while cooking.

1 Finely grate the rind from one lime and squeeze the juice from all of them.

2 Split the cardamom pods and remove the seeds. Crush with a mortar and pestle or the back of a heavy-bladed knife.

SUMMER HERB MARINADE

• • •

Make the best use of summer herbs in this marinade. Try any combination of herbs, depending on what you have on hand, and use with veal, chicken, pork, lamb or salmon.

INGREDIENTS

large handful of fresh herb sprigs, e.g. chervil, thyme, parsley, sage, chives, rosemary, oregano
6 tablespoons olive oil
3 tablespoons tarragon vinegar
1 garlic clove, crushed
2 scallions, chopped
salt and freshly ground black pepper

SERVES 4

3 Place the meat or fish in a bowl and pour the marinade over it. Cover and set aside to marinate in a cool place for 4–6 hours.

4 Drain the meat or fish when you are ready to cook it on the grill. Use the marinade to baste the meat occasionally while cooking.

1 Discard any coarse stalks or damaged leaves from the herbs, then chop them very finely.

2 Add the chopped herbs to the remaining marinade ingredients in a large bowl. Stir to mix thoroughly.

Desserts

—⟨◆⟩—

At the end of a barbecue it's a lovely idea to use the lingering fire

to make a delicious fruity dessert. You can cook fruit to melting

tenderness by wrapping it in foil, including sugar, spices and a sprinkling

of liqueur in the parcel. To broil fruit, cut it into chunks and spear it on

skewers, or just lay large slices on the grill rack. Sprinkle it with sugar

to caramelize in the heat. The aroma is intoxicating: even those who

thought they couldn't eat another bite will be beguiled by it. Accompany

grilled fruit with a buttery, spicy sauce, crisp toasted brioche or freshly

made griddle cakes – and perhaps a scoop of whipped cream or

ice cream – to make a perfect end to the meal.

GRILLED APPLES ON CINNAMON TOASTS

• • •

*This simple, scrumptious dessert is best made with an enriched bread such as brioche,
but any light, sweet bread will do.*

INGREDIENTS

*4 sweet dessert apples
juice of ½ lemon
4 individual brioches or muffins
4 tablespoons melted butter
2 tablespoons raw sugar
1 teaspoon ground cinnamon
whipped cream or strained plain
yogurt, to serve*

SERVES 4

2 Cut the brioches or muffins into thick slices. Brush the slices with melted butter on both sides.

4 Place the apple and brioche slices on a medium-hot grill and cook them for 3–4 minutes, turning once, until they are beginning to turn golden brown. Do not allow to burn.

1 Core the apples and use a sharp knife to cut them into 3 or 4 thick slices. Sprinkle the apple slices with lemon juice and set them aside.

3 Mix together the sugar and ground cinnamon in a small bowl to make the cinnamon sugar. Set aside.

5 Sprinkle half the cinnamon sugar over the apple slices and brioche toasts and grill for another minute, until the sugar is sizzling and the toasts are a rich golden brown.

6 To serve, arrange the apple slices over the toasts and sprinkle them with the remaining cinnamon sugar. Serve hot, with whipped cream or yogurt, if desired.

PINEAPPLE WEDGES WITH RUM BUTTER GLAZE

• • •

Fresh pineapple is even more full of flavor when grilled, and this spiced rum glaze
makes it into a very special dessert.

INGREDIENTS
1 medium pineapple
2 tablespoons dark brown sugar
1 teaspoon ground ginger
4 tablespoons melted butter
2 tablespoons dark rum

SERVES 4

3 Soak 4 bamboo skewers in water for 15 minutes to prevent them from scorching on the grill. Push a skewer through each wedge, into the stalk, to hold the chunks in place.

4 Mix together the sugar, ginger, butter and rum and brush over the pineapple. Cook the wedges on the grill for 4 minutes; pour the remaining glaze over the top and serve.

1 With a large, sharp knife, cut the pineapple lengthwise into 4 wedges. Cut out and discard the central core.

2 Cut between the flesh and skin, to release the skin, but leave the flesh in place. Slice the flesh across and lengthwise to make thick chunks.

Cook's Tip
For an easier version, simply remove the skin and then cut the whole pineapple into thick slices and cook as directed.

BAKED BANANAS WITH SPICY VANILLA FILLING

• • •

Bananas are ideal for barbecue cooking, as they bake in their skins and need no preparation at all. This flavored butter adds richness; children may prefer melted chocolate, jam or honey.

INGREDIENTS

4 bananas
6 green cardamom pods
1 vanilla bean
finely grated rind of 1 small orange
2 tablespoons brandy or orange juice
4 tablespoons light brown sugar
3 tablespoons butter
crème fraîche or strained plain
yogurt, to serve

SERVES 4

1 Place the bananas, in their skins, on a hot grill and cook for 6–8 minutes, turning occasionally, until they are turning brownish black.

2 Meanwhile, split the cardamom pods and remove the seeds. Crush lightly with a mortar and pestle.

3 Split the vanilla bean lengthwise and scrape out the tiny seeds. Mix with the cardamom seeds, orange rind, brandy or juice, brown sugar and butter into a thick paste.

4 Using a sharp knife, slit the skin of each banana, then open out the skin and spoon in a little of the paste. Serve with a spoonful of crème fraîche or yogurt, if desired.

211

ORANGES IN MAPLE AND COINTREAU SYRUP

· · ·

*This is one of the most delicious ways to eat an orange, and a luxurious way to round off
a barbecue. For a children's or alcohol-free version, omit the liqueur.*

INGREDIENTS

*4 teaspoons butter, plus extra,
melted, for brushing
4 medium oranges
2 tablespoons maple syrup
2 tablespoons Cointreau or Grand
Marnier liqueur
crème fraîche or fromage frais,
to serve*

SERVES 4

2 Remove some shreds of orange
rind, to decorate. Blanch these, dry
them and set them aside. Peel the
oranges, removing all the white pith
and catching the juice in a bowl.

4 Tuck the foil up securely around
the oranges so that they keep their
shape, leaving the foil open at the top.

1 Cut 4 double-thickness squares of
aluminum foil, large enough to wrap
each of the oranges. Brush the center of
each square of foil with plenty of
melted butter.

3 Slice the oranges crosswise into
thick slices. Reassemble them and place
each orange on a square of baking foil.

5 Mix together the reserved orange
juice, maple syrup and liqueur and
spoon the mixture over the oranges.

6 Add a pat of butter to each parcel
and close the foil at the top to seal in
the juices. Place the parcels on a hot
grill for 10–12 minutes, until hot. Serve
with crème fraîche or fromage frais,
topped with the reserved shreds of
orange rind.

NECTARINES WITH MARZIPAN AND MASCARPONE

• • •

A luscious dessert that no one can resist—dieters may prefer to use low-fat cream cheese or plain yogurt instead of mascarpone.

INGREDIENTS

4 firm, ripe nectarines or peaches
3 ounces marzipan
5 tablespoons mascarpone cheese
3 macaroons, crushed

SERVES 4

1 Cut the nectarines or peaches in half and remove the pits.

2 Divide the marzipan into 8 pieces, roll into balls, using your fingers, and press one piece of marzipan into the pit cavity of each nectarine half.

Cook's Tip

Either nectarines or peaches can be used for this recipe. If the pit does not pull out easily when you halve the fruit, use a small, sharp knife to cut around it.

3 Spoon the mascarpone cheese on top of the fruit halves. Sprinkle the crushed macaroons over the mascarpone.

4 Place the fruit halves on a hot grill for 3–5 minutes, until they are hot and the mascarpone starts to melt. Serve immediately.

GRILLED STRAWBERRY CROISSANTS

° ° °

*The combination of crisp grilled croissants, ricotta cheese and sweet strawberry
preserves makes for a deliciously simple, sinful dessert.*

INGREDIENTS

4 croissants
1/2 cup ricotta cheese
1/2 cup strawberry preserves
or jam

SERVES 4

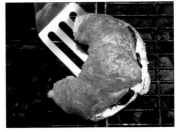

3 Top the ricotta with a generous
spoonful of strawberry preserves and
replace the top half of the croissant.

4 Place the filled croissants on a hot
grill and cook for 2–3 minutes, turning
once. Serve immediately.

1 On a chopping board, split the
croissants in half and open them out.

2 Spread the bottom half of each
croissant with a generous layer of
the ricotta cheese.

Cook's Tip

As an alternative to croissants,
try scones, brioches or muffins,
toasted on the grill.

GRIDDLE CAKES WITH MULLED PLUMS

• • •

These delectably light little pancakes are fun to make on the grill. They are served with a rich, spicy plum sauce.

INGREDIENTS

1¼ pounds red plums
6 tablespoons light brown sugar
1 cinnamon stick
2 whole cloves
1 piece star anise
6 tablespoons apple juice
cream or strained plain yogurt,
to serve

FOR THE GRIDDLE CAKES
½ cup all-purpose flour
2 teaspoons baking powder
pinch of salt
½ cup fine cornmeal
2 tablespoons light brown sugar
1 egg, beaten
1¼ cups milk
2 tablespoons corn oil

SERVES 6

1 Halve, pit and quarter the plums. Place them in a flameproof pan, with the sugar, spices and apple juice.

Cook's Tip

If you prefer, make the griddle cakes in advance, on the stove, and then simply heat them for a few seconds on the grill to serve with the plums.

2 Bring to a boil, then reduce the heat, cover the pan and simmer gently for 8–10 minutes, stirring occasionally, until the plums are soft. Remove the spices and keep the plums warm on the side of the grill.

3 For the griddle cakes, sift the flour, baking powder and salt into a large mixing bowl and stir in the cornmeal and brown sugar.

4 Make a well in the center of the dry ingredients and add the egg, then beat in the milk. Beat thoroughly with a whisk or wooden spoon to form a smooth batter. Beat in half the oil.

5 Heat a griddle or a heavy frying pan on a hot grill. Brush with the remaining oil, then drop tablespoons of batter onto it, allowing them to spread. Cook the griddle cakes for about a minute, until bubbles start to appear on the surface and the underside is golden brown.

6 Turn the cakes over and cook the other side for a minute more, or until golden. Serve the cakes hot from the griddle with a spoonful of mulled plums and cream or yogurt.

FRUIT KEBABS WITH CHOCOLATE FONDUE

Fondues are always lots of fun, and the delicious ingredients used here—fresh fruit, chocolate and marshmallow—will make this recipe a popular choice with children and adults alike.

2 Mix together the butter, lemon juice and ground cinnamon and brush the mixture generously over the fruit.

3 For the fondue, place the chocolate, cream and marshmallows in a small pan and heat gently, without boiling, stirring constantly until the mixture has melted and is smooth.

INGREDIENTS

2 bananas
2 kiwi fruit
12 strawberries
1 tablespoon melted butter
1 tablespoon lemon juice
1 teaspoon ground cinnamon

FOR THE FONDUE
8 ounces semisweet chocolate
½ cup light cream
8 marshmallows
½ teaspoon vanilla extract

SERVES 4

1 Peel the bananas and cut into thick chunks. Peel the kiwi fruit and quarter them. Thread the bananas, kiwi fruit and strawberries onto 4 wooden skewers. (Soak the skewers in water for 15 minutes beforehand to prevent them scorching on the grill.)

4 Cook the kebabs on a medium-hot grill, turning once, for 2–3 minutes, or until the fruit is golden. Stir the vanilla extract into the fondue. Empty the fondue into a small bowl and serve at once, with the fruit kebabs.

SPICED PEAR AND BLUEBERRY PARCELS
. . .

This fruity combination makes a delicious dessert for a hot summer evening.
You could substitute other berries for the blueberries if you prefer.

INGREDIENTS

4 firm, ripe pears
2 tablespoons lemon juice
1 tablespoon melted butter
1¼ cups blueberries
4 tablespoons light brown sugar
freshly ground black pepper

SERVES 4

3 Cut 4 squares of double-thickness aluminum foil, large enough to wrap the pears, and brush them with melted butter. Place two pear halves on each, cut sides up. Gather the foil up around them, to hold them level.

4 Mix the blueberries and sugar together and spoon them over the pears. Sprinkle with black pepper. Seal the edges of the foil over the pears and cook on a fairly hot grill for about 20–25 minutes.

1 Peel the pears thinly. Cut them in half lengthwise. Scoop out the core from each half, using a teaspoon and a sharp kitchen knife.

2 Brush the pears with lemon juice, to prevent them from discoloring.

Cook's Tip
To assemble in advance, line with a layer of waxed paper, as the acid in the lemon juice may react with the foil and taint the flavor.

FRESH FIGS WITH VANILLA CREAM

• • •

The ripeness of the figs will determine their cooking time. This is an ideal recipe for a barbecue because it is prepared on the grill and left to stand until you are ready to eat.

INGREDIENTS

2 cups dry white wine
⅓ cup clear honey
¼ cup sugar
1 small orange
8 whole cloves
1 pound fresh figs
1 cinnamon stick
sprigs of fresh mint, or bay leaves,
to decorate

FOR THE VANILLA CREAM
1¼ cups double cream
1 vanilla bean
1 teaspoon sugar

SERVES 6

1 Put the wine, honey and sugar in a heavy saucepan and heat gently on the grill or stovetop until the sugar dissolves.

2 Stud the orange with the cloves and add to the syrup with the figs and cinnamon. Cover and simmer very gently for 5–10 minutes, until the figs are tender. Transfer the contents of the pan to a serving dish and let cool.

3 Put ⅔ cup of the cream in a small saucepan with the vanilla bean. Bring almost to a boil, then allow to cool and infuse for 30 minutes. Remove the vanilla bean and mix the flavored cream with the remaining cream and sugar in a bowl. Whip lightly. Transfer to a serving dish.

4 Decorate the figs with mint or bay leaves and serve with the vanilla cream.

BAKED APPLES IN HONEY AND LEMON

° ° °

Tender, fluffy baked apples with a classic flavoring of lemon and honey make a simple, traditional dessert. Serve with custard or a spoonful of whipped cream, if you wish.

INGREDIENTS

4 medium cooking apples
1 tablespoon honey
grated rind and juice of 1 lemon
1 tablespoon butter, melted

SERVES 4

1 Remove the cores from the apples, leaving them whole. Cut four squares of double-thickness aluminum foil, to wrap the apples, and brush with butter.

2 With a cannelle or sharp knife, cut lines through the apple skin at regular intervals.

3 Mix together the honey, lemon rind, juice and butter in a small bowl.

4 Spoon the mixture into the apples and wrap in foil, sealing the edges securely. Cook on a hot grill for 20 minutes, until the apples are tender.

POACHED PEARS IN MAPLE AND YOGURT SAUCE

• • •

This elegant dessert is easier to make than it looks—poach the pears on the stove or grill when you cook the main course, and have the cooled syrup ready to add just before serving.

INGREDIENTS

6 firm pears
1 tablespoon lemon juice
1 cup sweet white wine
or cider
thinly pared rind of 1 lemon
1 cinnamon stick
2 tablespoons maple syrup
½ teaspoon arrowroot
⅔ cup strained plain yogurt

SERVES 6

1 Peel the pears, leaving them whole and with stalks. Brush with lemon juice to prevent them from discoloring. Use a potato peeler or small knife to scoop out the core from the bottom of each pear.

2 Place the pears in a wide, heavy pan and pour the wine over them, with enough cold water to almost cover the fruit. Add the lemon rind and cinnamon stick, and bring to a boil on the stove or, using a flameproof pan, on the grill. Reduce the heat, cover and simmer for 30 minutes, or until tender. Lift out the pears carefully.

3 Boil the remaining liquid, uncovered, until reduced to about ½ cup. Strain and add the maple syrup. Blend a little of the liquid with the arrowroot. Return to the pan and cook, stirring, until thick and clear. Allow to cool.

4 Slice each pear, leaving the slices attached at the stem end, and fan out on serving plates. Stir 2 tablespoons of the cooled syrup into the yogurt and spoon around the pears. Drizzle the pears with the remaining syrup and serve immediately.

CHOCOLATE MINT TRUFFLE FILO PARCELS

• ◦ •

These exquisite little parcels are utterly irresistible: there will be no leftovers. The use of fresh mint in the recipe gives a wonderfully fresh flavor.

2 Cut the filo pastry sheets into 3-inch squares and cover with a damp cloth to prevent them from drying out.

3 Brush a square of filo with melted butter, lay on a second sheet, brush again and place a spoonful of filling in the middle of the top sheet. Bring in all four corners and twist to form a purse shape. Repeat to make 18 parcels.

4 Place the filo parcels on a griddle or baking sheet, well brushed with melted butter. Cook on a medium-hot grill for about 10 minutes, until the filo pastry is crisp. Let cool, then dust lightly with sifted confectioners' sugar and then with sifted cocoa powder.

INGREDIENTS

1 tablespoon very finely chopped fresh mint
³/4 cup ground almonds
2 ounces semisweet chocolate, grated
¹/2 cup crème fraîche
2 dessert apples, peeled and grated
9 large sheets filo pastry
5¹/3 tablespoons butter, melted
1 tablespoon confectioners' sugar
1 tablespoon cocoa powder

MAKES 18 PARCELS

1 Mix the chopped fresh mint, almonds, grated chocolate, crème fraîche and grated apple in a large mixing bowl. Set aside.

OUTDOOR ENTERTAINING

———◦✦◦———

Everything tastes better out of doors, and picnics – whether in the
garden, at the beach or in a grassy meadow – are a great pleasure both
to organize and to take part in, as long as the weather is kind. If you
have a portable grill you can take it along with you and make the food
twice as exciting, but take care that you light it in a safe place and clear
up carefully afterwards. Food for grilling can be transported in its
marinade, all ready to be popped over the heat. Pack interesting dips
into plastic boxes, and take pitas or prepared vegetables to go with
them. Homemade quiches and pies will also help to satisfy healthy
outdoor appetites. This section also offers inspirations for special
summer meals and garden parties at home, including some original
and delicious ideas for party drinks.

VEGETABLES WITH TAPENADE AND HERB AIOLI

A beautiful platter of summer vegetables served with one or two interesting sauces makes an enticing and informal appetizer that is perfect for picnics, since it can all be prepared in advance.

INGREDIENTS

2 red bell peppers, cut into wide strips
2 tablespoons olive oil
8 ounces new potatoes
4 ounces green beans
8 ounces baby carrots
8 ounces young asparagus
12 quail eggs
fresh herbs, to garnish
coarse salt, for sprinkling

FOR THE TAPENADE
1¹/₂ cups pitted black olives
2-ounce can anchovy fillets, drained
2 tablespoons capers
¹/₂ cup olive oil
finely grated rind of 1 lemon
1 tablespoon brandy (optional)
freshly ground black pepper

FOR THE HERB AIOLI
5 garlic cloves, crushed
2 egg yolks
1 teaspoon Dijon mustard
2 teaspoon white wine vinegar
1 cup light olive oil
3 tablespoons chopped mixed fresh herbs, such as chervil, parsley and tarragon
2 tablespoons chopped watercress
salt and freshly ground black pepper

SERVES 6

1 To make the tapenade, finely chop the olives, anchovies and capers and beat together with the oil, lemon rind and brandy, if using. (Alternatively, lightly process the ingredients in a blender or food processor.)

2 Season with pepper and blend in a little more oil if the mixture seems very dry. Transfer to a serving dish.

3 To make the aïoli, beat together the garlic, egg yolks, mustard and vinegar. Gradually blend in the olive oil, a drop at a time, whisking well until thick and smooth.

4 Stir in the mixed herbs and watercress. Season with salt and pepper to taste, adding a little more vinegar if necessary. Cover with plastic wrap and chill until ready to serve.

> #### Cook's Tip
> Any leftover tapenade is delicious tossed with pasta or spread on warm toast. If you are making this dish as part of a picnic, allow the vegetables to cool before packing in an airtight container. Pack the quail eggs in their original box.

5 Brush the peppers with oil and cook on a hot grill or under a hot broiler until just beginning to char.

6 Cook the potatoes in a large pan of boiling, salted water until tender. Add the beans and carrots and blanch for 1 minute. Add the asparagus and cook for another 30 seconds. Drain the vegetables. Cook the quail eggs in boiling water for 2 minutes.

7 Arrange all the vegetables, eggs and sauces on a serving platter. Garnish with fresh herbs and serve with coarse salt, for sprinkling.

CRUDITES

· · ·

*Serve a colorful selection of raw vegetables as a quick and easy accompaniment
to aperitifs or as a refreshing appetizer for summer meals.*

RAW VEGETABLE PLATTER

INGREDIENTS

2 red or yellow bell peppers, sliced
lengthwise
8 ounces fresh baby corn,
blanched
1 head of chicory (red or white),
trimmed and leaves separated
6–8 ounces thin asparagus,
trimmed and blanched
small bunch radishes, trimmed
6 ounces cherry tomatoes
12 quail's eggs, boiled for
3 minutes, drained, refreshed and
peeled
aïoli or tapenade,
for dipping

SERVES 6–8

Arrange a selection of prepared
vegetables, chosen from the list above,
on a serving plate with your chosen
dip. Keep covered until ready to serve.

TOMATO AND CUCUMBER SALAD

INGREDIENTS

1 medium cucumber, peeled and
thinly sliced
2 tablespoons white wine vinegar
1/3 cup crème fraîche or
sour cream
2 tablespoons chopped fresh mint
4 or 5 ripe tomatoes, sliced
salt and freshly ground black
pepper

SERVES 4–6

Place the cucumber in a bowl, sprinkle
with a little salt and 1 tablespoon of the
vinegar and toss with 5 or 6 ice cubes.
Chill for 1 hour to crisp, then rinse,
drain and pat dry. Return to the bowl,
add the crème fraîche, mint, and
pepper and stir to mix well. Arrange
the tomato slices on a platter, sprinkle
with the remaining vinegar, and spoon
the cucumber slices into the center.

Cook's Tip

Any leftover vegetables can
be used in soups or stir-fries,
even if they have already
been dressed.

CARROT AND ORANGE SALAD

INGREDIENTS

1 garlic clove, crushed
grated rind and juice of 1 unwaxed
orange
2–3 tablespoons peanut oil
1 pound carrots, cut into very fine
julienne strips
2–3 tablespoons chopped fresh
parsley
salt and freshly ground black
pepper

SERVES 4–6

Rub the inside of a bowl with the garlic
clove, leaving the clove in the bowl.
Add the orange rind and juice, and
season with salt and freshly ground
pepper. Whisk in the peanut oil until
blended, then remove the garlic clove.
Add the carrots and half of the fresh
parsley and toss well to mix. Garnish
with the remaining parsley.

AIOLI

Put 4 peeled garlic cloves (more or less can be added, to taste) in a bowl with a pinch of salt, and crush with the back of a spoon. Add 2 egg yolks and beat for 30 seconds with an electric mixer, until creamy. Beat in 1 cup extra virgin olive oil, drop by drop. As the mixture thickens, the oil can be added in a thin stream. Thin the sauce with lemon juice, if necessary, and season to taste.

The aïoli can be kept for up to 2 days in the refrigerator; bring to room temperature and stir before serving.

TAPENADE

Put 7 ounces pitted black olives, 6 anchovy fillets, 2 tablespoons capers, rinsed, 1 or 2 garlic cloves, 1 teaspoon fresh thyme, 1 tablespoon Dijon mustard, the juice of half a lemon, freshly ground black pepper and, if

FROM TOP LEFT: Raw vegetable platter with aïoli, carrot and orange salad, tomato and cucumber salad.

you like, 1 tablespoon brandy in a food processor and process for 15–30 seconds, until smooth, scraping down the sides of the bowl. With the machine running, pour in 4–6 tablespoons extra virgin olive oil to make a smooth paste. Store in an airtight container.

FALAFEL

• • •

These North African fritters are traditionally made using dried fava beans, but chickpeas are more readily available. Serve in warmed pita bread, with salad and garlicky yogurt.

INGREDIENTS

3/4 cup dried chickpeas
1 large onion, roughly chopped
2 garlic cloves, roughly chopped
4 tablespoons roughly chopped fresh parsley
1 teaspoon cumin seeds, crushed
1 teaspoon coriander seeds, crushed
1/2 teaspoon baking powder
salt and freshly ground black pepper
oil for deep-frying

SERVES 4

1 Put the chickpeas in a large bowl and cover with plenty of cold water. Let soak overnight.

2 Drain the chickpeas and cover with fresh water in a saucepan. Bring to a boil and boil rapidly for 10 minutes. Reduce the heat and simmer for about 1 hour, or until soft. Drain.

3 Place in a food processor with the onion, garlic, parsley, cumin, coriander and baking powder. Season to taste. Process to form a firm paste.

4 Shape the mixture into walnut-size balls, using your hands, and flatten them slightly. In a deep pan, heat 2 inches of oil until a little of the mixture sizzles on the surface. Fry the falafel in batches until golden. Drain on paper towels and serve.

Cook's Tip
Although they can be fried in advance, falafel are at their best served warm. Wrap them in foil or pack them in an insulated container to take them on picnics, or keep them warm on the edge of the grill until needed.

HUMMUS BI TAHINA

• • •

*Blending chickpeas with garlic, lemon and oil makes a deliciously creamy purée to serve
as a dip with crudités or warmed pita bread.*

INGREDIENTS

*3/4 cup dried chickpeas
juice of 2 lemons
2 garlic cloves, sliced
2 tablespoons olive oil, plus extra
to serve
2/3 cup tahini (sesame paste)
salt and freshly ground black
pepper
cayenne pepper, to serve
flat-leaf parsley, to garnish*

SERVES 4–6

1 Put the chickpeas in a large bowl and cover with plenty of cold water. Let soak overnight.

2 Drain the chickpeas and cover with fresh water in a pan. Bring to a boil and boil rapidly for 10 minutes. Reduce the heat and simmer for about 1 hour, or until soft. Drain.

3 Process the chickpeas to a purée in a food processor. Add lemon juice, garlic, oil, cayenne pepper and tahini and blend until creamy.

4 Season the chickpea purée with plenty of salt and freshly ground black pepper and transfer to a serving dish. Drizzle the purée with olive oil and sprinkle lightly with cayenne pepper. Serve the dip garnished with a few flat-leaf parsley sprigs.

Cook's Tip

If you do not have time to soak dried chickpeas, canned chickpeas can be used instead. Allow two14-ounce cans and drain them thoroughly.

TOMATO AND CHEESE TARTS
· · ·

These crisp little tartlets look impressive but are actually very easy to make.
They are best eaten fresh from the oven.

INGREDIENTS
3 sheets filo pastry
1 egg white
6 ounces cream cheese
handful of fresh basil leaves
4 small tomatoes, sliced
salt and freshly ground black
pepper

MAKES 12

1 Preheat the oven to 400°F. Brush
the sheets of filo pastry lightly with egg
white and cut into 4-inch squares.

2 Layer the squares in twos, in
12 tartlet pans. Spoon the cream cheese
into the pastry shells. Season with
ground black pepper and top with
fresh basil leaves.

3 Arrange the tomatoes on the tarts,
season and bake for 10–12 minutes,
until the pastry is golden. Serve warm.

Cook's Tip
Use halved cherry tomatoes
for the tarts, if you prefer.

TANDOORI CHICKEN STICKS
• • •

These aromatic chicken pieces are traditionally baked in the special clay oven known as a tandoor. They are equally delicious served hot or cold, and make irresistible barbecue food.

2 To prepare the marinade, place all the ingredients in a food processor and process until smooth. Pour into a shallow dish.

3 Freeze the chicken breasts for 5 minutes to firm them, then slice in half horizontally. Cut the slices into ¾-inch strips and add to the marinade. Toss to coat well. Cover with plastic wrap and chill for 6–8 hours or overnight.

4 Drain the chicken pieces and arrange on a rack, scrunching up the chicken slightly to make wavy shapes. Cook on a hot grill for 4–5 minutes, until brown and cooked through, turning once. Alternatively, arrange on a foil-lined baking sheet and cook under a hot broiler. Serve hot, threaded on toothpicks or short skewers, with the yogurt dip. For a picnic, allow to cool and pack into a box.

1 For the cilantro yogurt, combine all the ingredients in a bowl. Season, cover and chill until ready to serve.

HAM PIZZETTAS WITH MELTED BRIE AND MANGO

• • •

These little individual pizzas are topped with an unusual but very successful combination of smoked ham, Brie and juicy chunks of fresh mango.

INGREDIENTS

2 cups white bread flour
1/4-ounce envelope active
dry yeast
2/3 cup warm water
4 tablespoons olive oil

FOR THE TOPPING
1 ripe mango
5 ounces smoked ham, sliced
wafer-thin
5 ounces Brie cheese, diced
12 yellow cherry tomatoes,
halved
salt and freshly ground black
pepper

SERVES 6

1 In a large bowl, stir together the flour and yeast, with a pinch of salt. Make a well in the center and stir in the water and 3 tablespoons of the olive oil. Stir until thoroughly mixed.

Cook's Tip
It's important to flatten out the dough rounds quite thinly and to cook them fairly slowly, or they will not cook evenly. To save time, you could use an 11-ounce package of pizza-dough mix.

2 Turn the dough out onto a floured surface and knead it for about 5 minutes, or until smooth.

3 Return the dough to the bowl and cover it with a damp cloth or oiled plastic wrap. Set the dough aside in a warm place for about 30 minutes, or until it is doubled in size and springy to the touch.

4 Divide the dough into 6 pieces and roll each piece into a ball. Flatten out with your hand and use your knuckles to press each piece of dough into a round about 6 inches in diameter, with a raised lip around the edge.

5 Halve, pit and peel the mango and cut it into small dice. Arrange with the ham on top of the pizzettas. Top with cheese and tomatoes and sprinkle with salt and ground black pepper.

6 Drizzle the remaining oil over the pizzettas. Place them on a medium-hot grill and cook for 8 minutes, until golden brown and crisp underneath.

OYSTER AND BACON BROCHETTES

. . .

Six oysters per person make a good appetizer, served with the seasoned oyster liquor to trickle over the skewers. Alternatively, serve nine per person as a main course, accompanied by a salad.

INGREDIENTS

36 oysters
18 thin-cut slices lean bacon
1 tablespoon paprika
1 teaspoon cayenne pepper
freshly ground black pepper
celery leaves and red chilies,
to garnish

FOR THE SAUCE
1/2 fresh red chili, seeded and very finely chopped
1 garlic clove, crushed
2 scallions, very finely chopped
2 tablespoons finely chopped fresh parsley
liquor from the oysters
juice of 1/4–1/2 lemon, to taste
salt and freshly ground black pepper

SERVES 4–6

2 Push the knife in and cut the muscle, holding the shell closed. Pour the liquor into the bowl. Cut the oyster free. Discard the drained shells.

3 For the sauce, mix the chili, garlic, scallions and parsley into the oyster liquor and sharpen to taste with lemon juice. Season with salt and pepper and transfer to a serving dish.

4 Cut each bacon slice across the middle. Season the oysters lightly with paprika, cayenne and freshly ground black pepper and wrap each one in half a bacon slice, then thread them onto skewers. Cook on a hot grill for about 5 minutes, turning frequently, until the bacon is crisp and brown. Garnish with celery leaves and red chilies and serve with the sauce.

1 Open the oysters over a bowl to catch their liquor for the sauce. Wrap your left hand (if you are right-handed) in a clean dish towel and cup the deep shell of each oyster in your wrapped hand. Work the point of a strong, short-bladed knife into the hinge between the shells and twist firmly.

TURKEY ROLLS WITH GAZPACHO SAUCE
· ◦ ·

This Spanish-style recipe uses quick-cooking turkey cutlets, but you could also cook veal scallops in the same way.

INGREDIENTS
4 turkey breast cutlets
1 tablespoon tomato pesto
4 chorizo sausages
1 tablespoon olive oil
salt and freshly ground black pepper

FOR THE GAZPACHO SAUCE
1 green bell pepper, chopped
1 red bell pepper, chopped
3-inch piece of cucumber
1 medium tomato
1 garlic clove
3 tablespoons olive oil
1 tablespoon red wine vinegar

SERVES 4

1 To make the gazpacho sauce, place the peppers, cucumber, tomato, garlic, 2 tablespoons of the olive oil and the vinegar in a food processor and process until almost smooth. Season to taste with salt and ground black pepper.

2 If the turkey breast cutlets are too thick, place them between two sheets of clear film and beat them with the side of a rolling pin, to flatten them slightly.

3 Spread the pesto over the turkey, place a chorizo on each piece and roll up firmly.

4 Slice the rolls thickly and thread them onto skewers. Brush with olive oil and cook on a medium grill for 10–12 minutes, turning once. Serve with the gazpacho sauce.

CHICKEN, MUSHROOM AND CILANTRO PIZZA

• • •

Shiitake mushrooms add an earthy flavor to this colorful pizza, while fresh chili and chili-flavored olive oil give it a hint of spiciness. Cook the pizza on the grill or in the oven.

INGREDIENTS

3 tablespoons olive oil
12 ounces skinned chicken breast fillets, cut into thin strips
1 bunch scallions, sliced
1 fresh red chili, seeded and chopped
1 red bell pepper, cut into thin strips
3 ounces fresh shiitake mushrooms, sliced
3–4 tablespoons chopped fresh cilantro
1 round of pizza dough, 10–12 inches in diameter
1 tablespoon chili oil
5 ounces mozzarella cheese
salt and freshly ground black pepper

SERVES 3–4

2 Pour off any excess oil, then set aside to let the chicken mixture cool.

3 Stir the fresh cilantro into the cooled chicken mixture in the wok.

4 Brush all over the top of the pizza-dough round with the chili oil.

5 Spoon on the chicken mixture and drizzle with the remaining olive oil.

6 Grate the mozzarella and sprinkle it over the pizza. Cook the pizza on a medium-hot grill for about 15–20 minutes, until the crust is crisp and golden and the cheese is bubbling. Serve the pizza immediately.

1 Heat 2 tablespoons olive oil in a wok or large frying pan. Add the chicken, scallions, chili, red pepper and mushrooms and stir-fry over high heat for 2–3 minutes, until the chicken is firm but still slightly pink inside. Season to taste.

MEDITERRANEAN QUICHE

• • •

*This quiche forms the ideal basis for a hearty picnic feast. The strong Mediterranean flavors of
tomatoes, peppers and anchovies complement the cheese pastry beautifully.*

INGREDIENTS

FOR THE PASTRY
2 cups all-purpose flour
pinch of salt
pinch of dry mustard
8 tablespoons (1 stick) butter,
chilled and diced
2 ounces Gruyère, grated
salt and freshly ground black
pepper

FOR THE FILLING
2-ounce can anchovy fillets, drained
1/4 cup milk
2 tablespoons French mustard
3 tablespoons olive oil
2 large Spanish onions, peeled and
sliced
1 red bell pepper, very finely sliced
3 egg yolks
1½ cups heavy cream
1 garlic clove, crushed
6 ounces sharp Cheddar cheese,
grated
2 large tomatoes, thickly sliced
2 tablespoons chopped fresh basil,
to garnish

SERVES 6–8

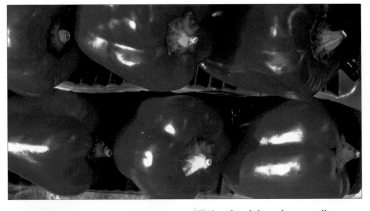

2 Add the Gruyère and process
again briefly. Add enough ice water to
make a stiff dough: the dough will be
ready when it forms a ball. Wrap the
dough in plastic wrap and chill in the
refrigerator for at least 30 minutes.

3 Meanwhile, make the filling.
Soak the anchovies in the milk for
about 20 minutes to make them less
salty. Pour off the milk. Heat the olive
oil in a frying pan and cook the onions
and red pepper until they soften.

1 To make the pastry, place the flour,
salt and mustard in a food processor,
add the butter and process the mixture
until it resembles fine bread crumbs.

4 In a bowl, beat the egg yolks,
cream, garlic and Cheddar cheese
together; season with salt and pepper.

5 Preheat the oven to 400°F. Roll out
the chilled pastry and use it to line a
9-inch quiche pan with a removable
bottom. Spread the mustard over the
pastry and chill for another 15 minutes.

6 Arrange the tomatoes in a layer in
the pastry crust. Top with the onion
and pepper mixture and the anchovy
fillets. Pour on the egg mixture. Bake
for 30 minutes. Serve warm or at room
temperature, sprinkled with fresh basil.

Cook's Tip
Leave the quiche in its pan if
you are packing it for a picnic.

CHICKEN AND APRICOT FILO PIE

• • •

The filling for this pie has a Middle Eastern flavor—ground chicken combined with apricots,
bulgur wheat, nuts and spices. It both looks and tastes spectacular.

INGREDIENTS

1/2 cup bulgur
6 tablespoons butter
1 onion, chopped
1 pound ground chicken
1/4 cup dried apricots, finely
chopped
1/4 cup blanched almonds, chopped
1 teaspoon ground cinnamon
1/2 teaspoon ground allspice
1/4 cup strained plain yogurt
1 tablespoon snipped fresh chives,
plus extra to garnish
2 tablespoons chopped fresh
parsley
6 large sheets filo pastry
salt and freshly ground black
pepper

SERVES 6

1 Preheat the oven to 400°F. Put
the bulgur in a large bowl with 1/2
cup boiling water. Allow the bulgur
to soak for 5 minutes, until the water
is absorbed.

2 Heat 2 tablespoons of the butter in
a pan and fry the onion and chicken
until pale golden. Stir in the apricots,
almonds and bulgur and cook for
another 2 minutes. Remove from the
heat and stir in the cinnamon, allspice,
yogurt, chives and parsley. Season to
taste with salt and pepper.

3 Melt the remaining butter. Unroll
the filo pastry and cut into 10-inch
rounds. Keep the pastry rounds covered
with a clean, damp dish towel to
prevent them from drying out.

4 Line a 9-inch removable-bottomed
tart pan with 3 pastry rounds, brushing
each with butter as you layer them.
Spoon in the chicken mixture and cover
with 3 more pastry rounds, brushed
with melted butter as before.

5 Crumple the remaining rounds
and place on top of the pie. Brush with
any remaining butter. Bake the pie for
about 30 minutes, until the pastry is
golden brown and crisp. Serve hot or
cooled, garnished with fresh chives.

CHICKEN WITH FRESH HERBS AND GARLIC

* * *

A whole chicken can be roasted on a spit on the grill. This marinade keeps the flesh moist and delicious, and the fresh herbs add summery flavors.

INGREDIENTS

4½-pound free-range chicken
finely grated rind and juice of
1 lemon
1 garlic clove, crushed
2 tablespoons olive oil
2 fresh thyme sprigs
2 fresh sage sprigs
6 tablespoons unsalted butter,
softened
salt and freshly ground black
pepper

SERVES 4

1 Season the chicken well. Mix the lemon rind and juice, crushed garlic and olive oil together and pour them over the chicken. Let marinate in the refrigerator for at least 2 hours.

Cook's Tip

If roasting the chicken in the oven, preheat the oven to 450°F and reduce the heat to 375°F after 10 minutes. If you are roasting a chicken to serve cold, cooking it in foil helps to keep it succulent—open the foil for the last 20 minutes to brown the skin, then close it as the chicken cools.

2 Place the herbs in the cavity of the bird and smear the butter over the skin. Season well. Cook the chicken on a spit on the grill for 1½–1¾ hours, basting with the marinade, until the juices run clear when a thigh is pierced with a skewer. Let the bird rest for 15 minutes before carving.

PEPPER STEAK
• • •

This easy, rather indulgent bistro classic can be put together in a matter of minutes for an intimate summer supper in the garden. The creamy sauce helps to balance the heat of the pepper.

INGREDIENTS

2 tablespoons black peppercorns
2 tenderloin or boneless sirloin
steaks, about 8 ounces each
1 tablespoon butter
2 teaspoons olive oil
3 tablespoons brandy
2/3 cup whipping cream
1 garlic clove, finely chopped
salt, if necessary

SERVES 2

1 Place the black peppercorns in a sturdy plastic bag. Crush the peppercorns with a rolling pin or meat pounder until they are crushed to medium-coarse pepper.

2 Put the steaks on a chopping board and trim away any excess fat, using a sharp kitchen knife. Press the pepper firmly onto both sides of the meat, to coat it completely.

3 Melt the butter with the olive oil in a heavy frying pan over medium-high heat. Add the meat and cook for 6–7 minutes, turning once, until cooked to your liking. Transfer the steaks to a warmed platter or plates and cover to keep warm.

4 Pour in the brandy to deglaze the pan. Allow the brandy to boil until it has reduced by half, scraping the bottom of the pan, then add the whipping cream and garlic. Bubble gently over medium-low heat for about 4 minutes, or until the cream has reduced by about one-third. Stir any accumulated juices from the meat into the sauce, taste and add salt as necessary. Serve the steaks hot, with the sauce.

PORK WITH MARSALA AND JUNIPER

° ° °

*Sicilian marsala wine gives savory dishes a rich, fruity and alcoholic tang. The pork is fully
complemented by the flavor of the sauce in this quick and luxurious dish.*

INGREDIENTS

*1 ounce dried cèpe or porcini
mushrooms*
4 pork scallops
2 teaspoons balsamic vinegar
8 garlic cloves
1 tablespoon butter
3 tablespoons marsala
several rosemary sprigs
10 juniper berries, crushed
*salt and freshly ground black
pepper*

SERVES 4

1 Put the dried mushrooms in a
large bowl and just cover with hot
water. Let stand for 20 minutes
to allow the mushrooms to soak.

2 Brush the pork with 1 teaspoon of
the vinegar and season with salt and
pepper. Put the garlic cloves in a small
pan of boiling water and cook for 10
minutes, until soft. Drain and set aside.

3 Melt the butter in a large frying
pan. Add the pork and fry quickly until
browned on the underside. Turn the
meat over and cook for 1 minute more.

4 Add the marsala, rosemary sprigs,
drained mushrooms, 4 tablespoons of
the mushroom water, the garlic cloves,
juniper berries and the remaining
balsamic vinegar.

5 Simmer gently for 3–5 minutes,
until the pork is cooked through.
Season lightly and serve hot.

STUFFED ROAST LOIN OF PORK

· · ·

This recipe uses fruit and nuts as a stuffing for roast pork in the Catalan style. It is full of flavor and is very good served cold, making an excellent centerpiece for a summer buffet or a picnic.

INGREDIENTS

4 tablespoons olive oil
1 onion, finely chopped
2 garlic cloves, chopped
1 cup fresh bread crumbs
4 dried figs, chopped
8 pitted green olives, chopped
1/4 cup sliced almonds
1 tablespoon lemon juice
1 tablespoon chopped fresh parsley
1 egg yolk
2-pound boned loin of pork
salt and freshly ground black pepper

SERVES 4

1 Preheat the oven to 400°F, or prepare the grill. Heat 3 tablespoons of the oil in a pan, add the onion and garlic, and cook gently until softened. Remove the pan from the heat and stir in the bread crumbs, figs, olives, almonds, lemon juice, chopped fresh parsley and egg yolk. Season to taste with salt and ground black pepper.

2 Remove any string from the pork and unroll the belly flap, cutting away any excess fat or meat to enable you to do so. Spread the stuffing over the flat piece and roll it up, starting from the thick side. Tie at intervals with string.

3 Pour the remaining olive oil into a roasting pan and put in the pork, or arrange on the spit of the grill. Roast for 1 hour and 15 minutes, or until the juices from the meat run clear.

4 Remove the pork from the oven or the spit and, if serving hot, let it rest for 10 minutes before carving into thick slices. If serving cold, wrap the meat in foil to keep it moist until you carve it.

LAMB CASSEROLE WITH GARLIC AND BEANS

This Spanish-influenced recipe makes a substantial meal when served with potatoes.
Fava beans add color and texture to the dish.

INGREDIENTS

3 tablespoons olive oil
3–3½ pounds lamb fillet, cut
into 2-inch cubes
1 large onion, chopped
6 large garlic cloves, unpeeled
1 bay leaf
1 teaspoon paprika
½ cup dry sherry
4 ounces shelled fresh or frozen
fava beans
2 tablespoons chopped fresh parsley
salt and freshly ground black
pepper

SERVES 6

3 Add the garlic, bay leaf, paprika and sherry. Season to taste and bring to a boil. Cover and simmer gently for 1½ hours, until tender.

4 Add the fava beans to the casserole and cook for another 10 minutes. Stir in the chopped fresh parsley just before serving.

1 Heat 2 tablespoons olive oil in a large flameproof casserole. Add half the meat and brown well on all sides. Transfer to a plate. Brown the rest of the meat in the same way and remove from the casserole.

2 Heat the remaining oil in the pan, add the onion and cook for about 5 minutes, until soft. Return the meat to the casserole.

RED MULLET WITH LAVENDER

. . .

Cook a fish dish with a difference by adding lavender to red mullet for a wonderful, aromatic flavor. Sprinkle some lavender flowers on the coals too, to give a delightful perfumed ambience.

INGREDIENTS

4 red mullet, scaled, gutted and cleaned
2 tablespoons olive oil

FOR THE MARINADE
3 tablespoons fresh lavender flowers or 1 tablespoon dried lavender leaves, roughly chopped
roughly chopped rind of 1 lemon
4 scallions, roughly chopped
salt and freshly ground black pepper

SERVES 4

1 Place the fish in a shallow dish. Mix the ingredients for the marinade and pour over the fish. Cover the fish with plastic wrap and let marinate in the refrigerator for at least 3 hours.

2 Remove the fish from the marinade and brush it with olive oil. Cook the fish on a hot grill for 10–15 minutes, turning once and basting with olive oil as they cook.

248

SALMON STEAKS WITH OREGANO SALSA

• • •

This combination of salmon with piquant tomato works incredibly well. The barbecue gives the salmon an exquisite flavor. Served hot or cold, this is an ideal dish for a summer lunch.

INGREDIENTS
1 tablespoon melted butter
4 salmon steaks, about 8 ounces
each
1/2 cup white wine
freshly ground black pepper

FOR THE SALSA
2 teaspoons chopped fresh
oregano, plus sprigs to garnish
4 scallions, trimmed
8 ounces ripe tomatoes, peeled
2 tablespoons extra virgin olive oil
1/2 teaspoon sugar
1 tablespoon tomato paste

SERVES 4

1 Butter 4 squares of double-thickness aluminum foil. Put a salmon steak on each and add a little wine and a grinding of black pepper. Wrap the salmon steaks loosely in the foil, sealing the edges securely. Cook on a medium-hot grill for 10 minutes, until just tender. If serving the steaks hot, keep them warm.

2 Put the chopped fresh oregano in a food processor and chop it very finely. Add the scallions, tomatoes and remaining salsa ingredients. Pulse until chopped but not a smooth purée.

3 Serve the salmon hot or cold with the salsa, garnished with a sprig of fresh oregano.

HERBAL PUNCH

• • •

This refreshing party drink will have people coming back for more, and it is an original non-alcoholic choice for drivers and children.

INGREDIENTS

2 cups honey
7 pints water
2 cups freshly squeezed
lemon juice
3 tablespoons fresh rosemary
leaves, plus extra to decorate
8 cups sliced strawberries
2 cups freshly squeezed
lime juice
7½ cups
sparkling mineral water
ice cubes
3–4 scented geranium leaves,
to decorate

SERVES 30 PLUS

1 Combine the honey, 4 cups water, one-eighth (¼ cup) of the lemon juice and the fresh rosemary leaves in a saucepan. Bring to a boil and heat, stirring constantly, until the honey is dissolved. Remove from the heat and allow to stand for about 5 minutes. Strain into a large punch bowl and set aside to cool.

2 Press the strawberries through a fine sieve into the punch bowl, add the rest of the water and lemon juice, the lime juice and the sparkling mineral water. Stir gently to combine the ingredients. Add the ice cubes just 5 minutes before serving, and float the geranium and rosemary leaves on the surface.

MINT CUP

• • •

Mint is a perennially popular flavoring, and this delicate cup is a wonderful mixture with an intriguing taste. It is the perfect summer drink to serve with meals outdoors.

INGREDIENTS

handful of fresh mint leaves
1 tablespoon sugar
crushed ice
1 tablespoon lemon juice
³/₄ cup grapefruit juice
2¹/₂ cups chilled
tonic water
mint sprigs and lemon slices,
to decorate

SERVES 4–6

1 Crush the mint leaves with the sugar and put into a pitcher. Fill the pitcher to the top with crushed ice.

2 Add the lemon juice, grapefruit juice and tonic water. Stir gently to combine the ingredients and decorate with mint sprigs and slices of lemon.

STRAWBERRY AND MINT CHAMPAGNE

This is a simple concoction that makes a bottle of champagne or sparkling white wine go much further. It tastes very special on a hot summer evening.

INGREDIENTS
1¼ pounds strawberries
6–8 fresh mint leaves
1 bottle champagne or sparkling white wine
fresh mint sprigs, to decorate

SERVES 4–6

1 Purée the strawberries and fresh mint leaves in a food processor.

2 Strain through a fine sieve into a large bowl. Half-fill a glass with the mixture and top up with champagne or sparkling wine. Decorate with a sprig of fresh mint.

MELON, GINGER AND BORAGE CUP

Melon and ginger complement each other magnificently. If you prefer, you can reduce or leave out the powdered ginger—the result is milder but equally delicious.

INGREDIENTS
½ large honeydew melon
4 cups ginger ale
1 teaspoon powdered ginger
borage sprigs with flowers, to decorate

SERVES 6–8

1 Discard the seeds from the half melon and scoop the flesh into a food processor. Blend the melon to a purée.

2 Pour the purée into a large jug and top up with ginger ale. Add powdered ginger to taste. Pour into glasses and decorate with borage.

INDEX

· · ·

NOTES

NOTES

NOTES

NOTES

NOTES

NOTES

NOTES

NOTES